Genocide:
A World History

The New Oxford World History

Genocide:
A World History

Norman M. Naimark

OXFORD
UNIVERSITY PRESS

OXFORD
UNIVERSITY PRESS

Oxford University Press is a department of the University of Oxford. It furthers
the University's objective of excellence in research, scholarship, and education
by publishing worldwide. Oxford is a registered trade mark of Oxford University
Press in the UK and certain other countries.

Published in the United States of America by Oxford University Press
198 Madison Avenue, New York, NY 10016, United States of America.

Library of Congress Cataloging-in-Publication Data
Names: Naimark, Norman M., author.
Title: Genocide : a world history / Norman M. Naimark.
Description: New York, NY : Oxford University Press, [2017] | Series: New Oxford world
history | Includes bibliographical references and index.
Identifiers: LCCN 2016019771 | ISBN 978–0–19–976526–3 (pbk. : alk. paper) |
ISBN 978–0–19–976527–0 (hardback : alk. paper)
Subjects: LCSH: Genocide—History.
Classification: LCC HV6322.7 .N348 2017 | DDC 364.15/109—dc23 LC record available
at https://lccn.loc.gov/2016019771

Hardback printed by Bridgeport National Bindery, Inc., United States of America

*Frontispiece: Photos of tortured and murdered victims of the Cambodian genocide
at the Tuol Sleng Genocide Museum in Phnom Penh, Cambodia, housed in a former
prison used by the Khmer Rouge regime.* Photo by Mark Garten/UN Photo.

Contents

Editors' Preface

This book is part of the New Oxford World History, an innovative series that offers readers an informed, lively, and up-to-date history of the world and its people that represents a significant change from the "old" world history. Only a few years ago, world history generally amounted to a history of the West—Europe and the United States—with small amounts of information from the rest of the world. Some versions of the "old" world history drew attention to every part of the world *except* Europe and the United States. Readers of that kind of world history could get the impression that somehow the rest of the world was made up of exotic people who had strange customs and spoke difficult languages. Still another kind of "old" world history presented the story of areas or peoples of the world by focusing primarily on the achievements of great civilizations. One learned of great buildings, influential world religions, and mighty rulers but little of ordinary people or more general economic and social patterns. Interactions among the world's peoples were often told from only one perspective.

This series tells world history differently. First, it is comprehensive, covering all countries and regions of the world and investigating the total human experience—even those of so-called peoples without histories living far from the great civilizations. "New" world historians thus share in common an interest in all of human history, even going back millions of years before there were written human records. A few "new" world histories even extend their focus to the entire universe, a "big history" perspective that dramatically shifts the beginning of the story back to the big bang. Some see the "new" global framework of world history today as viewing the world from the vantage point of the Moon, as one scholar put it. We agree. But we also want to take a close-up view, analyzing and reconstructing the significant experiences of all of humanity.

This is not to say that everything that has happened everywhere and in all time periods can be recovered or is worth knowing, but that there is much to be gained by considering both the separate and interrelated stories of different societies and cultures. Making these connections is still another crucial ingredient of the "new" world history. It emphasizes connectedness and interactions of all kinds—cultural, economic, political, religious, and social—involving peoples, places, and processes. It makes comparisons and finds similarities. Emphasizing both the comparisons and interactions is critical to developing a global framework that can deepen and broaden historical understanding, whether the focus is on a specific country or region or on the whole world.

The rise of the new world history as a discipline comes at an opportune time. The interest in world history in schools and among the general public is vast. We travel to one another's nations, converse and work with people around the world, and are changed by global events. War and peace affect populations worldwide, as do economic conditions and the state of our environment, communications, and health and medicine. The New Oxford World History presents local histories in a global context and gives an overview of world events seen through the eyes of ordinary people. This combination of the local and the global further defines the new world history. Understanding the workings of global and local conditions in the past gives us tools for examining our own world and for envisioning the interconnected future that is in the making.

Bonnie G. Smith
Anand Yang

Introduction

Genocide has been a part of human history from its very beginnings. There is little reason to think that our prehistoric forebears were either more or less civilized than ourselves when confronting and eliminating other peoples and suspected enemies. Extended families, clans, and tribes routinely engaged in genocidal actions against their rivals, just as ancient empires and modern nation-states enacted their murderous hatred for imagined or real enemies in mass killing. Over the ages, genocide has had both internal and external dimensions. Political leaders of societies small and large, primitive and modern, have turned against internal groups—tribal, ethnic, religious, social—and sought their elimination as a way to preserve privilege, avoid dissidence, consolidate power, and accumulate wealth. They have also conquered and dominated neighboring (or distant) territories for a variety of imperial purposes and have killed and suppressed, as well as co-opted, native peoples of those regions in order to dominate them and seize their land and resources.

Any consideration of the world history of genocide must deal with the question of definition, for it is crucial in understanding the special character of genocide as the "crime of crimes" in order to distinguish it from other terrible atrocities against human beings that have been committed over the centuries. Genocide is a different category of crime from, for example, war crimes, which were originally defined by the Hague Convention of 1898 and then further developed by the Nuremberg Tribunal in 1946 and the Geneva Convention of 1949. These include such war-specific crimes as looting, the murder of hostages, the use of gas, and the killing of prisoners of war. Genocide also differs from "crimes against humanity," which the Treaty of Rome (1998) classifies as murder, extermination, enslavement, depopulation or forcible transfer of population, torture, and a variety of sexual crimes, including rape.[1] Genocide has its own provenance deriving from the thinking and activism of the Polish Jewish lawyer Raphael Lemkin. Contemporary international society owes the concept of genocide to Lemkin and to his involvement in the promulgation of the 1948 U.N. Convention on the Prevention and Punishment of Genocide. Lemkin was also the first to develop a world historical approach to genocide.

Raphael Lemkin was born in 1900 in Russian Poland and studied law in Lwów (now Lviv) and Heidelberg during the 1920s.[2] Even as a young lawyer in Warsaw at the beginning of the 1930s, Lemkin was fixated on mass killing as an international crime. The Armenian genocide of 1915 attracted his attention, as did the Simele massacre of Assyrian Christians in northern Iraq in 1933. He became convinced that the only way to prevent or deter similar crimes was to employ international law. As a result, he authored a paper, presented to a League of Nations–sponsored meeting of international lawyers in Madrid in 1933, which defined two crimes that should be proscribed by international law. The first of the crimes he called "barbarism," which was Lemkin's first stab at a concept that he later named "genocide." "Whosoever, out of hatred towards a racial, religious or social collectivity, or with the view of the extermination thereof, undertakes a punishable action against the life, bodily integrity, liberty, dignity or economic existence of a person belonging to that collectivity, is liable, for the crime of barbarity." Lemkin also created the idea of what might be considered cultural genocide, which he called at the time "vandalism." "Whosoever, either out of hatred towards a racial, religious or social collectivity, or with a view to the extermination thereof, destroys its cultural or artistic works will be liable for the crime of vandalism."[3] The League took little note of Lemkin's ideas and soon had to face the same Nazi threat that changed Lemkin's life forever.

On September 1, 1939, Hitler attacked Poland and proceeded to murder tens of thousands of Poles and drive the country's Jews into ghettos, where they soon began to die in huge numbers from hunger and disease. Lemkin saw the writing on the wall and fled to Sweden. Eventually, he made his way to the United States, where his first job was teaching at Duke University Law School. Soon thereafter, he worked in Washington, D.C., for the Carnegie Peace Foundation and with the War Department as a consultant. In Washington, he continued to collect material on the Nazi occupation of Europe, including the laws and edicts that established the foundations for Nazi repressive policies in Europe. In 1944, Lemkin published his research in a book called the *Axis Rule in Occupied Europe*. Here, Lemkin described the derivation of the term "genocide." "By 'genocide' we mean the destruction of a nation or of an ethnic group. This new word, coined by the author to denote an old practice in its modern development, is made from the ancient Greek word *genos* (race, tribe) and the Latin *cide* (killing), thus corresponding in its formation to such words as tyrannicide, homicide, infanticide, etc."[4] Clearly, Lemkin had found a term that resonated with Western public opinion as it eventually confronted the Holocaust and other monstrous crimes of mass killing. Lemkin's experiences with the Nazis and his justifiable fears about what had happened to his own family in Poland—many of its members were killed—served to focus much of his efforts on publicizing the desperate plight of the Jews.

A tireless lobbyist, Lemkin was at Nuremberg in the late fall of 1946, trying to convince the prosecutors to include genocide in the indictments against the Nazi war criminals who stood trial. But the international court was much more interested in the condemnation of aggressive war than in the mass murder of the Jews or of anyone else. Lemkin then worked the corridors of the newly formed United Nations to promote the passage of an international law against genocide. Here he had more success, as representatives of the Soviet Union, Poland, and Yugoslavia, as well as of some other countries, joined forces with Jewish groups to encourage the General Assembly to pass a resolution in December 1946 condemning the crime of genocide "whether it is committed on religious, racial, political, *or any other grounds*" and to charge the U.N.'s 6th (Legal) committee with drafting a convention against genocide.[5] In the subsequent negotiations about formulating a convention on genocide, the Soviets and their allies, as well as others, insisted that social and political groups be dropped completely from the language of the document. Thus, the Convention on the Prevention and Punishment of Genocide, unanimously adopted by the General Assembly of the United Nations on December 9, 1948, with Lemkin in the gallery, famously defined genocide as a variety of "acts committed with the intent to destroy, in whole or in part a national, ethnical, racial or religious group, as such."[6]

What is often missed in the reading of the Convention is that its preamble supported Lemkin's contention that genocide was ubiquitous in the history of mankind: "Recognizing that in all periods of history genocide has inflicted great losses on humanity." In fact, Lemkin engaged in a wide-ranging project of his own, researching and writing about the worldwide historical dimensions of genocide.

The definition of genocide proffered by Lemkin in his 1944 book and elaborated upon in the 1948 Convention remains to this day the fundamental definition accepted by scholars and the international courts in their work on genocide both past and present. It is the definition that is used in this study, though amended to take into account Lemkin's original idea that the targeted elimination of social and political groups should be included in genocide. The adjectival form *genocidal* is used here to mean "like or pertaining to genocide," though not necessarily the equivalent of genocide itself.

The definition of genocide in this book also relies on the subsequent evolution of the term's meaning as developed by a series of international tribunals.[7] For example, international jurisprudence has found it more fruitful to focus on the centrality of mass killing in evaluating genocide than in some of the interrelated aspects of genocide proscribed in the Convention, such as: "Imposing measures intended to prevent births within the group" or "Forcibly transferring children of the group to another group." These acts, separate from mass killing, have generally not been accepted themselves in the courts as genocide, but have been considered in combination with intentional mass murder to demonstrate genocidal intentions, methods, and effects.

It is easy to understand the frustration of some scholars, lawyers, and policymakers with arguments about whether a particular set of events is genocide or not because the very use of the word influences how we approach the issue of intervening in a crisis situation. Arguments about applying the term also pervade the historical claims of many peoples for recognition of the murderous tragedies or assaults on cultures that befell their particular ethnic group or nation. In both contexts, it is important that the definition of genocide be neither too broad and labile nor too narrow and constricted. Some commentators would like to see genocide subsumed—along with "crimes against humanity" and "war crimes"—under the general category of "atrocities."[8] But atrocities can include a wide variety of crimes, ranging from those committed by drug gangs against innocent schoolchildren to those that can be carried out even by individual soldiers or groups of soldiers in a situation of occupation or civil war. Similarly, war crimes and crimes against humanity can and should be distinguished from genocide, though they clearly overlap at the margins.

There are also many who find the word *genocide* too general and too widely applied. They would prefer what they consider more precise words like *sociocide, politicide, ethnocide, democide,* even *genderocide,* depending on the circumstances and the precise character of the target population. But *genocide* has stood the test of time in a way very few recently invented terms have. The scholarly and legal literature is rich enough to establish a common meaning and common understanding, even if claims of genocide are sometimes abused by special pleading, and governments and individuals deny genocide through definitional wrangling. Lemkin found a term for intentional mass murder that was powerful and resonant, effective and lasting.

This book also assumes that genocide is a worldwide historical phenomenon that originates with the beginning of human society. Cases of genocide need to be examined, as they occur over time and in a variety of settings. They are also sometimes linked with one another as events in a single narrative in which earlier cases can influence later ones. In some cases, one can speak of direct examples; in some, these influences are embedded in specific cultures. The Old Testament serves as a foundational text for genocide in Western civilization, a dramatic script that reverberates through the ages in commentaries and literary representations that reflect the patterns of destruction demanded by the Hebrew God. Thucydides' writings on the Athenian conquest of Melos and on Spartan forms of warfare and destruction similarly established philosophical arguments about the character of genocide—as distinct from warfare—that found their way into Roman, medieval, and early modern texts.[9] Perhaps no classical case of genocide has remained imprinted in modern Western memory as profoundly as the Roman destruction of Carthage, immortalized in the speeches of Cato and the writings of Virgil.

Contemporaneous writings about the genocidal Spanish conquest of the New World referred repeatedly to the ancients. Meanwhile, the Spanish conquest became the model for policies of later colonial governments, just as opponents of the extirpation of native peoples in Australia and North America often mentioned the writings of Bartolemé de Las Casas, the notable Dominican critic of Spanish brutality in the new world.

One of the first observers of linkages between episodes of genocide was Hannah Arendt, who noted the influence of colonial brutality and racism on the development of the genocidal policies of Hitler in Europe.[10] The widespread killing of native peoples in the colonies, French, British, Italian, and especially German, translated in some fashion into mass murder during World War II.[11] A number of historians have noted some continuity in personnel and policies between the German military's attempts to eliminate the Herero and Nama peoples in Southwest Africa (1904–1907), their role as advisers in the Armenian genocide (1915), and the Wehrmacht's role in the Holocaust.[12] Hitler stated to his generals on the eve of his onslaught against Poland and the Poles: "Who, after all, speaks today about the annihilation of the Armenians?" In the same speech, Hitler also chose to cite the positive example of Genghis Khan as an empire builder. Hitler's message was clear: the German war leadership should not shy away from killing large numbers of Poles and Jews in the attack.[13]

Not all genocides are the same. Some are carried out in a matter of days or weeks; others can take decades. Some involve millions of people; others thousands. Some are highly centralized; others more decentralized and sporadic. Every case of genocide is in some ways unique, but it is also true that they can be grouped spatially and temporally into more or less similar kinds of murderous events. Historical periods do make a difference in the types and character of the killing involved. Obviously, we also know a lot less about genocides in the distant past and from geographically isolated regions and the peripheries of the large empires without a relatively rich written record. Still, there is a remarkable—indeed, frightening—similarity in genocidal violence over the past three millennia of human history.

CHAPTER 1

The Ancient World

It is impossible to know with certainty whether the pre-history of humankind produced genocidal situations. Archeologists and anthropologists conclude from the examination of excavated burial sites that prehistoric people massacred each other, and in some cases, engaged in various forms of torture and cannibalism. It is sometimes asserted that the forerunners of modern humans, *Homo sapiens*, physically exterminated the last vestiges of Neanderthal groups. Burial sites also reveal evidence of mass killing by tribes and clans from the Stone Age to the end of the Bronze Age, which would take us up to approximately 1200 BCE. With that said, prehistoric burial sites are so scattered and rare that it is difficult to come to any hard-and-fast conclusions about genocide as inherent to human civilization before written records.

The first reports of genocide during the ancient world come to us from written testimonies that describe events said to have taken place centuries earlier. The Hebrew Bible (the Old Testament), written in pieces at the end of the seventh century BCE, during the reign of King Josiah, and putatively describing events as far back as 1200 BCE, cannot, of course, be used as a historical source that accurately portrays the life of the ancient Hebrews. Like book II of Virgil's *Aeneid*, which describes the legendary destruction of Troy by the Achaeans around 1200 BCE, the Hebrew Bible should be considered a literary creation, a mixture of fact and fiction that served the religious and political needs of the society in which it was composed. The usefulness of archeology is severely limited when considering, in particular, the character and extent of mass killing in the ancient biblical period.

The historical veracity of Thucydides' *History of the Peloponnesian Wars* and its recounting of the destruction of Melos (416–415 BCE), and of Roman accounts of the razing of Carthage (c. 140 BCE) is easier to defend. Yet they, too, were written and read, as was the Hebrew Bible, as ways to interpret the challenges and problems that confronted the authors, their audiences, and their civilizations, rather than as history.

These accounts were also used by future generations of leaders—even centuries and millennia later—to justify and to model their own proclivities toward genocide. The kinds of tropes and metaphors that infused the Bible and the "classics" were absorbed into a worldwide discourse on killing and elimination.

The exodus of the Jews from Egypt, their wandering in the desert, and their conquering of the land of Israel serve as the central narrative trajectory of the Old Testament. As their God led the Hebrews on this journey, he demanded obedience from his chosen people in exchange for supporting their claims against more numerous and powerful enemies who sought to bring them harm. Most prominently, the Amalekites, a semi-nomadic people of the desert, earned the wrath of God by attacking the Israelites. Moses sent Joshua and his army to fight and vanquish them, ensuring victory by standing on a hill holding his staff with outstretched arms, supported by his brother Aaron and brother-in-law Hur. But military victory was not enough for the Hebrew God, who said to Moses: "Write this for a memorial in a book, and rehearse it in the ears of Joshua: for I will utterly put out the remembrance of Amalek from under heaven." Moses said: "The LORD will have war with Amalek from generation to generation."[1]

In completing the narrative of the destruction of the Amalekites, the book of Samuel tells one of the most powerful stories of genocide in the Old Testament and, indeed, in human history. The prophet Samuel came to Saul, who was to be anointed the first king of united Israel. (Saul is said to have lived from 1079 to 1007 BCE.) Samuel explained that God ordered Saul to attack and kill the Amalekites because of their transgressions against the Israelites when the latter had escaped from Egypt. "Now go and smite Amalek, and utterly destroy all that they have, and spare them not; but both man and woman, infant and suckling, ox and sheep, camel and ass."[2] According to the book of Samuel, Saul then assembled two hundred thousand foot soldiers and ten thousand soldiers of Judah, no doubt a wildly exaggerated number, and attacked the Amalekites in their capital city. In doing so, Saul "utterly destroyed all of the people with the edge of the sword," sparing only their noble king, Agag, and allowing his people to keep the best of the enemy's livestock. These exceptions to elimination infuriated the Hebrew God; Saul had not obeyed his orders. As a result of God's displeasure, Samuel, in the presence of God, "hewed Agag in pieces" and removed Saul as king, replacing him eventually with David.[3] Saul had not followed God's injunction to finish the job of genocide.

Later, King David himself pursued campaigns against the Amalekites, burning their cities, killing men and boys, and taking their women captive. He was able at one point to rescue his two wives from them, as well as plunder the wealth they had taken from Judea. When he had caught up with the raiders, "David smote them from the twilight even unto the evening of the next day: and there escaped not a man of them, save four hundred young men, which rode upon camels, and fled."[4]

The Amalekites were not the only people of the region to suffer the wrath of God and his chosen people. The Hebrew God spoke to the Israelites of numbers of peoples—the Amorites, the Hittites, the Perizzites, the Canaanites, the Hivites, and Jebusites—whom he promised to "blot out." As the Old Testament states, "Thou shalt smite them, and utterly destroy them.... Ye shall destroy their altars, and break down their images."[5] Here, the Hebrew God was speaking both of genocide and of cultural genocide. These peoples had the potential of corrupting the Israelites with their religions and customs, and therefore had to be eliminated. "They shall not dwell in your land, less they make thee sin against me; for if thou serve their gods, it will surely be a snare unto thee."[6] The language of mass killing in Deuteronomy is even stronger. When God "delivers them [the peoples who resided in Canaan] before thee; thou shalt smite them, and utterly destroy them. Thou shalt make no covenant with them, nor shew mercy unto them."[7] Deuteronomy also enjoins the Israelites to commit cultural genocide: "Ye shall destroy their altars, and break down their images. . . and burn their graven images with fire."[8] If this were not enough, God promised to destroy the "survivors and fugitives" of these peoples by sending the pestilence against them.

The Hebrew word *herem* is used in the Old Testament to describe this and other cases of what could be called "utter destruction." It had the completeness of both material and metaphysical elimination.[9] The fate of the resident peoples within the boundaries of the new home of the Israelites was thus sealed: "thou shalt save alive nothing that breatheth."[10] Peoples in more distant lands, where the Israelites exerted no direct claims of hegemony, could be treated more leniently. If their towns were willing to capitulate, then their inhabitants could serve in "forced labor." If not, then the towns would be besieged, the men put to death, and the women, children, and livestock taken for spoils.[11]

The destruction of Jericho is perhaps the best-known story of battle in the Bible, though few discuss it as genocide. In the Hebrews' first encounter in their new lands, sometimes dated to 1200 BCE, Joshua was sent out by God to destroy the Canaanite stronghold of Jericho, "City of Palm Trees," just west of the Jordan River. In the colorful Old

Testament rendition of the battle, Joshua and his army marched around the city walls seven times led by his trumpeters, whose blasts from their horns led to the collapse of the walls. In typical fashion, Joshua's army then completely destroyed "all that was in the city, both man and woman, young and old, and ox, and sheep, and ass, with the edge of the sword."[12] Jericho was burned to the ground and leveled. Joshua ended his campaign by pronouncing a chilling oath forbidding the rebuilding of the city:

> And Joshua adjured them at that time
> Saying, cursed be the man before the Lord,
> That riseth up and buildeth this city Jericho:
> He shall lay the foundation thereof in his first born,
> And in his youngest son shall he set up the gates of it.[13]

There is scant archaeological or related textual evidence to support any of these putative episodes of genocide described in the Hebrew Bible as historical events.[14] But more important than the historicity of the described destruction of peoples and towns is the fact that the biblical rendition of genocide reveals what men and women of antiquity believed was possible, even likely, in the relations between nations, while at the same time setting precedents, patterns, and norms for the future. The leaders of the Hebrews—Moses, Samuel, Saul, David, and Joshua—implemented the will of God to commit mass murder. Sometimes, the killing was in righteous retribution for alleged acts committed against the Hebrews. But most often, peoples were attacked and eliminated because they lived in the land that God had promised to the Hebrews. Those eliminated were blamed for their own fate, a widespread phenomenon in mass killing that has repeated itself over the centuries. Sometimes, women and children were spared as slaves and concubines, or even taken as wives.

Cultural genocide also was an important part of the biblical story. Not only were whole peoples wiped out, their temples were torn down and their cities completely destroyed and set aflame. To be sure, none of these actions described in the Hebrew Bible are unique to the Israelites in the ancient world (or later). In fact, scholars of ancient Israel note that judging from their archaeological remains, the neighbors of the Hebrews, the Philistines, Phoenicians, Arameans, Ammonites, Moabites, and Edomites, engaged in many of the same kinds of activities.[15] The Hebrew Bible, too, can be better understood in its use of particular literary tropes by comparing it to other great historical myth-laden documents from the region and time: Amenemope, Gilgameš, and Ugarit.[16]

But most important to the subsequent history of genocide were the ideas and images that made their way through the millennia and influenced readers to conceive of and think about mass killing in its biblical proportions, whether or not it happened as described. The shocking moral imperative associated with the Hebrew God's insistence on mass murder also has imbued the history of genocide in cultures associated with the Judeo-Christian tradition from the very beginning to the modern era.

Genocide was also no stranger to ancient Greek civilization, stretching from the Mycenaean period of the second millennium BCE through the Classical and Hellenistic ages, ending in 146 BCE with the Roman conquest. Here, the fundamental model for destruction comes from the accumulated mythological tales and stories about the Trojan War set down in the works by Homer and other Greek poets some time in the eighth and seventh centuries BCE. (The Trojan War is said by classical Greeks, even the prudent Thucydides, to have taken place some time in the thirteenth or twelfth centuries BCE.) In the *Iliad*, Homer's descriptions of the last year of the siege of Troy, at the end of nearly ten years of episodic warfare, are bloody and filled with cruelty. Agamemnon, king of Mycenae and commander of the Achaean forces arrayed against Troy, admonishes his brother Menelaus (husband of the abducted Helen):

> My dear Menelaus, . . . why are you so chary of taking men's lives? Did the Trojans treat you as handsomely as that when they stayed in your house? No; we are not going to leave a single one of them alive, down to the babies in their mothers' wombs—not even they must live. The whole people must be wiped out of existence, and none be left to think of them and shed a tear.[17]

The Achaeans then slaughtered the heroic defenders of Troy. No one was allowed to surrender; Trojan fighters were killed; the women were raped and murdered; their children were thrown from the ramparts. Homer depicts a great and wealthy city whose people were killed and whose wealth was despoiled and seized. In the end, the city was burned to the ground with many of its inhabitants perishing in the flames. Virgil's *Aeneid*, which tells the story of the last Trojan, Aeneas, and his flight from Asia Minor to found the city of Rome, similarly paints a picture of rivers of blood at Troy. "Who could speak of such slaughter? Who could weep tears to match that suffering? . . . The bodies of the dead lay through all its streets and houses and the sacred shrines of its gods. . . . Everywhere there was fear, and death in many forms."[18] Whether this rendition of the Achaeans' successful subjugation of Troy (what the archeologists call Troy VII) was actually a matter of genocide or not is no more historically certain than the Hebrew Bible's description of Joshua's murderous destruction of Jericho. But like the events of the Bible, the bloody violence of the Trojan War was recalled, remembered, and absorbed by subsequent civilizations that read and recited these lines of poetry and relived their beauty and pain.

Thucydides wrote his *History of the Peloponnesian War* over the course of the twenty-seven year conflict between Athens and Sparta at the end of the fifth century BCE. Justifiably considered the first "critical historian," Thucydides had participated as an admiral in that war and drew important lessons in military history and international politics from the long and bitter struggle. In the Melian Dialogue, which took place in the sixteenth year of the war, Thucydides narrates a story of genocide that highlights the "rational" character of its ancient origins. The Athenians used their powerful navy to establish dominion one by one over the Aegean islands. The Athenian empire demanded submission of the island of Melos, a colony of the Lacedemonians (Spartans). In discussion with the Melian leaders, the Athenians emphasized that they were not interested in justifying their demand for submission because of the historical rights of their empire or "because of the wrong you have done us" (the Melians had observed strict neutrality in the war). Instead, they considered it in their interests to establish hegemony in the islands, especially in those islands that had been colonies of Sparta. If Melos did not submit, the Athenians would destroy its inhabitants.

Questions of identity also played an important role in the conflict with the Melians. The subjugation of the island was important to the Athenian leaders in order to look strong and impregnable in the eyes of their own people, as well as in the eyes of their enemies. The Athenians explained that their subjects would think of them as weak if they let the Melians maintain their independence, adding that "the fact that you are islanders and weaker than others rendering it all the more important that you should not succeed in baffling the masters of the sea." The Melians, hoping in vain for help from the Lacedemonians or for a concession from the Athenians in a peace treaty, refused to submit. The outcome was predetermined, writes Thucydides: the Athenians "put to death all the grown men whom they took, and sold the women and children for slaves, and subsequently sent out five hundred colonists and inhabited the place themselves."[19]

One can assume that this kind of action on the part of the Athenians was matched in kind by its rival Sparta, a militaristic, slave-based society of warriors and conquerors. Thucydides notes, for example, that during the Peloponnesian War, the Spartans "butchered as enemies all whom they took on the sea, whether allies of Athens or neutrals." They massacred the populations of enemy cities that they besieged and conquered. When the city of Hysiae fell to the Spartans, they killed "all the freemen that fell into their hands." The Spartans' cruelty to their slaves (Helots) was unbounded. Domestic upheavals and rebellions were met by the most fearsome punishments.[20] In the cases of both the Athenians and Spartans in Thucydides, there is a palpable sense of the alien nature of the enemies that they conquered and slayed, and, in the most extreme cases, committed genocide against.

It seems that every great empire has drawn sustenance and energy from its rivalry with another; this was as true of Rome and Carthage as it was of Athens and Sparta. The Romans were the legendary heirs of Aeneas, the last of the Trojans, while the Carthaginians were the descendants of the maritime Phoenicians, who founded the city of Carthage on the site of modern Tunis, in roughly 1000 BCE. The first two Punic Wars between Rome and Carthage, 264–241 BCE and 218–202 BCE, saw battles rage across the western Mediterranean, with the Carthaginians seizing control of all of North Africa and Spain and, with Hannibal's remarkable campaign across the Alps, occupying substantial parts of the boot of Italy, though never conquering Rome. By the end of the Second Punic War (201 BCE), Carthage had been forced to withdraw from Sicily and Italy, and was confined to a relatively small corner of North Africa. Still, the city was large—by some estimates it had as many as 750,000 inhabitants—and enterprising, trading across the Mediterranean and even into the Atlantic with what is now Great Britain.

Carthage could live with Rome; Rome could not tolerate Carthage. The Mediterranean, in the Romans' view, was simply not big enough for both of them.[21] Marcus Porcius Cato, the Censor, was said to have concluded every one of his speeches in the Roman Senate with the words *Delenda est Carthago* ("Carthage is to be eliminated"). His was a burning hatred for this perceived poisonous thorn in the side of Rome. The ostensible *casus belli* for the Third Punic War, which the Roman Senate—and not just Cato—had been urging, were the hostilities between the Carthaginians and the Numidian king Masinissa, who made demands on Carthage that were supported by Rome. When Carthage sought to punish the Numidians by force, Rome declared war on Carthage in 149 BCE. In response to the Roman invasion, the Carthaginians surrendered, until it was clear that the Roman demands were that the city be completely destroyed, while its inhabitants were to be driven out and not allowed to build new homes within ten miles of the sea. At this point, those Carthaginians who had urged defiance won the day and began a two-year defense of the city under Roman siege.

Finally, in early 146 BCE, the Roman legions under Scipio Aemilianus broke through the city walls and fought street by street with the defenders. Many thousands of Carthaginians were slaughtered before the city was totally defeated. The survivors were sold into slavery, and true to Cato's injunctions, the city was burned to the ground. One still finds references to the undocumented "salting" of the city by the Romans, so that it could never rise again. Whether true or not, the story captures the spirit of the Romans' genocidal intentions in Carthage. The people would be eliminated; their city would be eradicated; and their culture would not be tolerated. From the time of the defeat, the Roman Senate also referred no longer to the territories of North Africa as Carthage but merely as a *provincia* called "Africa."[22] The memory of Carthage was likewise to be removed. Like the legendary destruction of Troy that led to the creation of Rome, Carthage would be sacrificed for the complete dominion of Rome in the Mediterranean.

The narratives of destruction thus sketched seem far away from the world in which we live and the genocides about which we speak. The salting of the earth, the taking of slaves and concubines, the prominence of motifs of revenge, the animal sacrifices to the gods (and to God), and the brutality of life itself seem alien to modernity and its prosecution of war and mass murder, not to mention its daily rhythms of work and play. Yet, the character of genocide has many similarities across time. Armies of men kill identifiable groups of human beings, including women, children, and noncombatants, at the command of their political leaders, who often invoke ideologies, gods, and God in their arguments for destruction. The killing is intentional, total, and eliminationist.

Ancient genocides were often committed beyond the ill-defined borders of the perpetrators' own lands, in part to seek new territory for domination, as in the case of the Athenians and Romans, but also to eliminate potential enemies from territory claimed by invaders, in the case of the ancient Israelites. Retribution for alleged past injuries also serves as a justification for genocide, as in the case of the Romans in Carthage and the Israelites with the Amalekites. Imperial glory, pride, and feelings of superiority permeate campaigns of genocide. The Athenians, whose claims of pure rational thinking in Thucydides' rendition of the attack on Melos, barely conceal the hubris of an empire insulted by any opposition and ready to assert its own visions of hegemony through mass killing.

Cultural genocide cuts a deep groove into the patterns of ancient war and conflict. The cities and cultures of Jericho, Troy, and Carthage were looted and burned to the ground. Nothing was to be left behind: no temples, no statues, no signs of past glory. When spared, the women and children were forcibly assimilated into the cultures of the perpetrators. In the rare cases when men and boys survived the onslaught, they were forced to serve in the armies of the victors. It is impossible to know how many cultures and peoples were eliminated through genocide and cultural genocide in the ancient world. But the numbers were surely substantial.

CHAPTER 2

Warrior Genocides

"They came, they sapped, they burnt, they slew, they plundered and they departed."[1] This description of the Mongol conquests by a contemporary indicates that throughout its history genocide has had a very close relationship to war. Even during periods of peace, the threat of war or the ostensible need to prepare for war can instigate genocidal situations. War is not a necessary precondition for genocide, and genocide does not necessarily occur during war. Still, genocide is most often associated with wartime intentions, policies, and actions. This is as true of ancient times as of the present. In fact, the general decrease in the incidence of war and civil conflict over the ages no doubt contributes to the decreasing incidence of genocide.[2]

The close connection between war and genocide makes it sometimes extremely difficult to distinguish between the military destruction of enemies during wartime and genocide. The idea of war as a confined and pristine conflict between two sets of armies that meet in battle captures only a part of what war is and means. Of course, there is a history of battlefield confrontations and of strategic and tactical decisions, not to mention the issues of morale and equipment that go into their resolution. But the home front also plays a crucial role in war.

Almost always, civilian casualties are heavy, and women, children, and the elderly are intimately involved. From ancient wars through the Napoleonic campaign at the beginning of the nineteenth century (sometimes considered the first "total" war), and the horrors of World War I and World War II, the boundary between military and home front became quickly permeable. It is sometimes said that only in the twentieth century did war take higher civilian casualties than military. But surely this would be hard to argue if one takes into account the starvation, disease, and epidemics unleashed by warfare in earlier periods.

In the warrior societies of the Middle Ages, the killing of enemies in combat and genocidal campaigns are frequently very hard to separate. In the West, notions of chivalry on the battlefield mixed with the barbarous readiness to eliminate whole groups of enemies, often with religious ("Christian") justifications as the backdrop. In the east, Mongol warriors also slaughtered enemies, sometimes as whole groups, because of perceived slights or resistance to the inevitability of Mongol overlordship. The twenty-first-century observer has to be careful not to make the particularities of a distant world, in this case that of the Crusaders or the Mongol warriors, blend too easily with those of their modern counterparts. But the wholesale massacres of civilians that the warrior societies of the past engaged in also should not be separated from the genocides of the modern world in any hard-and-fast way.

The Mongol empire, which dominated huge swaths of territory between the Pacific Ocean in the east and Central Europe in the west, the lands of Arabia and India in the south and Siberia and the Russian tundra in the north, was one of the most successful political formations in the history of humankind. During its greatest geographical reach, in the thirteenth and fourteenth centuries, it was the largest contiguous empire in world history and held sway over one hundred million people. Yet its origins and the spirit of its rulers derived from that of a nomadic people, who excelled in horsemanship and in fighting and were little attached to industry or urban life and culture. The empire also developed an unusual ability to use the talents of other peoples for its administration and its commercial needs, and to exploit the abilities of craftsmen and technicians of war among the many tribes and nations that it conquered. With its superior system of communications and intelligence, and its military prowess, based both on the careful organization of its army and the self-sufficiency of its horseback warriors, the Mongol empire swept before it much more economically sophisticated and culturally developed kingdoms and empires.

Historians evaluate the Mongol empire from different perspectives. Some underscore the positive dimensions of the Pax Mongolica, within which commerce, trade, and ideas flowed freely, including along the Silk Route, the fabled link between Europe and Asia that carried Marco Polo, among others, from Renaissance Italy to Beijing and back. Generally, the Mongols were tolerant of religious differences and, as such, promoted the interaction between the culturally rich communities of faith in Central and South Asia, Europe and the Middle East.

The Mongols also held little interest in racial, ethnic, or linguistic distinctions, which in the end fostered communications and the mixing of peoples and cultures in their vast empire. Many of the khans' most trusted generals and officials represented a wide variety of nationalities and religions from Eurasia. Recent research on

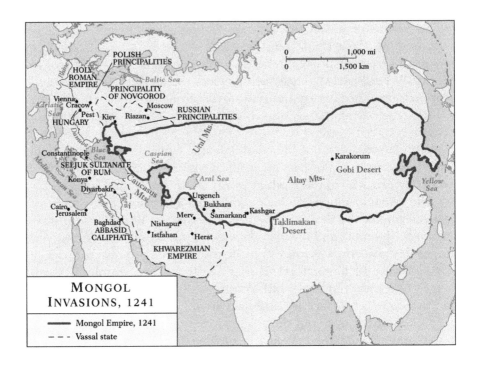

MONGOL
INVASIONS, 1241

——— Mongol Empire, 1241
– – – Vassal state

the presence of a dominant Y chromosome among one-eighth of the population of a larger Eurasian area indicates the extent to which the Mongol khans, descended from Genghis Khan, the first of the great Mongol leaders, intermarried with the royal families of conquered and absorbed territories, while taking in concubines of myriad races and nations.

Other historians emphasize the costs in human lives of the Mongol conquests. In two centuries of Mongol rule, more than 30 million people were killed in war and retribution.[3] The population of the Hungarian kingdom was halved by Mongol occupation, from 2 million to 1 million. In fifty years of Mongol rule, the population of China is also said to have been cut in half, from 120 million inhabitants to 60 million. But critics of these figures have noted that the Chinese were hard to count under Mongol census practices, thus making such numbers impossible to verify. There are also arguments about whether the "Mongol yoke," as it is still called in Russia, led to a similar depopulation and the impairment of economic and political development in the region inhabited by the East Slavs.

The Mongol empire owed its origins to a fairly obscure tribal chief, Temüjin, who managed by skillful diplomacy along with the force of arms to unite a number of Mongolian and Turkic tribes under his command. In 1206, already ruling a vast geographical territory in the center of Eurasia, Temüjin was named Genghis Khan—the "Fearless Leader."

The mass killing perpetrated by Genghis Khan and his warriors followed three distinct if overlapping templates. Not unlike the Athenians at Melos, one template presented the target people with the choice of either submitting to Mongol overlordship or facing complete destruction. This was the case of the Mongols' campaigns in Russia, where princely centers like Riazan and Suzdal were destroyed and Kiev was sacked before the Russians surrendered to the khan, paid the required tribute, and were absorbed into the Mongol legal realm. A single prince among the Russian princes was presented with the *iarlyk*, a contract that gave him the right to collect tribute from the other princedoms on behalf of the Mongols. In the case of dutiful payment, the Mongols left the Russians alone. That the principality of Moscow held the *iarlyk* for some time was crucial to its future role as the "gatherer" of the Russian lands.

The second template of Mongol violence faced those political entities, many in China and India, that decided to resist subjugation by military means. This was an unwise decision, since the Mongol military forces were usually far superior in preparation and fighting ability. Especially their horseback archers, organized in mobile cavalry units, were unmatched by any similar forces they encountered. The Mongols also easily absorbed military units from already conquered territories. Their siege tactics were highly developed, and they employed the most advanced technologies for constructing battering rams and flame-throwing artillery. Much of their technological know-how came from Chinese experts on gunpowder and weaponry. Wherever the Mongol armies went, they drafted talented experts into their own army engineering battalions.

Once the enemy was vanquished, the defeated men were usually separated into distinct groups. Highly valued craftsmen were often spared and sent back to the Mongolian capitals to ply their trades. (Later, during the Armenian genocide, the Ottomans sometimes spared Armenian craftsmen for similar reasons.) Women and children were given over to the Mongolian soldiers as slaves and wives and incorporated into Mongolian society. Everyone else was killed, often in groups of victims assigned for execution to individual Mongol soldiers. Several days after the massacres of their prisoners, Mongolian troops were sent back to the remnants of the destroyed cities to make sure that all those who might have survived or who had hidden were killed. After the Mongols had swept through the villages and towns of their enemies, "those abodes became a dwelling for the owl and the raven; in those places the screech-owls answer each other's cries, and in those halls the winds moan."[4] The Mongolian empire spread through sheer terror. What prince and population would be willing to resist the Mongols knowing that the fate of extermination awaited them?

There was also a third template for the killing that Genghis Khan and his successors perpetrated in Eurasia, and this was "total elimination." This form of Mongol mass killing can certainly be considered genocide, though it is important to reiterate that the Mongols did not attack groups because they hated or resented their religions or ethnicities. In this template, whole communities sometimes faced elimination at the hands of the Mongols because of a perceived slight or transgression. Genghis Khan and his successors did not tolerate those opponents who in one way or another insulted their honor. This pertained in particular to those communities that made the mistake of killing Mongolian chiefs or ambassadors, or in other ways demeaned Mongolian offers of peace. In these cases, whole cities were destroyed, including men, women, and children. However, unlike the cases of Carthage or Troy, the Mongols usually saw no reason for destroying the defeated cities themselves, though prominent architectural reminders of their civilizations and local sources of pride were indeed burned and demolished. In these cases, like so many in the history of genocide, the Mongols blamed their opponents for their own death and destruction.

The Persian-speaking and Islamic Khwarezmian empire, which was founded in Central Asia south of the Aral Sea around its capital of Samarkand, and included such remarkable centers of trade and civilizations as Bukhara and Urgench, quickly spread into the Iranian plateau, as well as the western parts of Afghanistan. The Shāh ʿAlāʾ ad-Dīn Muhammad of Khwarezmia (ruled 1200–20) defied the Mongols by rejecting their offers of a peace treaty and by humiliating and slaying their ambassadors. As a consequence, according to the well-informed Persian scholar and Mongol administrator, ʿAlāʾ al-Dīn ʿAṭā Malik Juvaynī, the major cities of Khwarezmia were attacked in a genocidal campaign that saw Samarkand, Bukhara, and Urgench brutally conquered and razed. The lands of Khwarezmia, especially those in what is contemporary Iran, were severely depopulated, as the Mongols destroyed agriculture lands (and turned them over to pasture for their animals) and trading towns. According to some scholars, it took until the modern era for the region to recover from the depopulation associated with the Mongol conquest.

The central cities of Khwarezmia were thought to be impregnable to invaders from the north and indeed defended themselves well. But the Khwarezmians could not stand up to the advanced siege equipment, as well as the superior military strength and high morale, of the Mongols. According to Juvaynī, the Mongols reneged on their promise to spare the Turkic soldiers defending the garrison in the capital of Samarkand and slaughtered them all. After the Mongols sent the best artisans and craftsmen to Mongolia, they order the people of the city to assemble on the outskirts, where they summarily executed them all, raising pyramids of skulls around the city as symbols of victory. Bukhara suffered a similar fate as the Khwarezmian capital. In both cities, the Mongols targeted and destroyed royal buildings.

In Urgench, after the Mongols gave the young women and children to their soldiers, they massacred the rest of the population according to established practice. Each Mongolian soldier was given the task of executing twenty-four men and women of Urgench, which, if true—and it is likely to be an exaggeration—would have meant a massacre of more than a million people. In Termez on the Oxus River, Juvaynī reported, "all the people, both men and women, were driven out into the plain, and divided in accordance with their [the Mongols'] usual custom, then they were all slain."[5]

The city of Merv (in contemporary Turkmenistan) fell in February 1221 to Tolui, Genghis Khan's youngest son, who is said to have massacred 700,000 persons while sparing some eighty craftsmen.[6] The city of Nishapur in present-day northeastern Iran was similarly targeted for Mongol vengeance. Here, the Mongols condemned the entire population to elimination because an arrow from the ramparts of the city struck and killed Genghis Khan's son-in-law. Per course, the Mongols piled the heads of men, women, and children in pyramids around the conquered town. Herat (in contemporary Afghanistan) was completely destroyed after a week of the killing of its inhabitants, as well as of some two thousand survivors of the Merv massacres who had taken refuge in the city.[7]

Killing and genocide also accompanied the Mongol incursions into Eastern Europe. Especially the invasion of the Hungarian kingdom in 1241 proved to be bloody and costly for the Magyars. The forebodings of the invasion already appeared to King Béla IV, several decades earlier. Russian nobles had come to Hungary warning of the Mongols' war-making prowess and their brutality. But no one really understood who the Mongols were or what, in the end, hit them.[8] The king himself received repeated messengers from Ögedei Khan, the favorite son and heir of Genghis Khan, to surrender his kingdom to the Mongols or suffer complete destruction. The nomadic Cumans had been defeated by the Mongols and sought refuge in Hungary under the king. Béla figured he could use the Cumans to help keep the unruly Hungarian magnates under control. He had the Cumans baptized and then incorporated them into the Hungarian estates system. But instead of improving the security of his kingdom, he managed to alienate further not only the magnates but also the Hungarian peasants, who were shocked at having to do obeisance to "barbarians" from the east. As a result, when the Mongols invaded under the leadership of Ögedei's son, Batu, the Hungarian lands were already in disarray.

As Batu's armies entered Hungary from the north, Master Roger, the great church chronicler and witness of the Mongol invasion, reports that the Mongol chieftain "began to burn down villages, and his word did not pardon sex or age, and he hastened as fast as he could against the king." Béla withdrew to Pest and refused to engage the Mongols, as they raided the countryside, burning and killing, in Master Roger's words, "as their inborn viciousness dictated." When the city of Vác was seized, the townspeople and peasants from the surrounding countryside took refuge in the church and the palace of the church, which was "fortified like a castle." But this did them no good. After the Mongols looted the church's treasury, "they completely burned in the fire all those whom they did not wish to kill by the sword; all the canons and other persons, ladies, and girls."[9]

Upon the urging of the church fathers to stop the depredations that were occurring throughout the Hungarian countryside, Béla finally marched out to meet the outnumbered Mongols in battle. But his nobles were disunited and some even wished for his defeat. The Cuman king had been killed by aroused Hungarian burghers, who thought he was responsible for the invasion. The Mongols surrounded Béla's army with archers and the Hungarians took very heavy casualties. As Master Roger puts it, "the Hungarian nation was slipping away," fleeing toward the Danube to seek respite from the conquerors. "The slaughter among both those fleeing on the broad road towards Pest and those who stayed with the army was so enormous, so many thousand men perished, that one cannot estimate it nor can one very well trust reports as the loss was so huge." The Mongols dismembered the bodies of those they caught and burned others to death who tried to take refuge in churches and villages along the way. Master Roger continues: "Corpses lay around as common as flocks of cattle or sheep or pigs standing on open ground to pasture or like stone cut for building in a quarry."[10]

The king of Hungary sought out the protection of the duke of Austria, who demanded large indemnities from him and in fact raided western Hungary for booty while the Mongols occupied the territory east of the Danube and continued their genocidal campaigns. The city of Oradea was seized, plundered, and burned down. Master Roger comments: "Having collected the booty, they killed men and women, commoners and nobles alike, on the streets, houses, and fields. What more? They pardoned neither sex nor age."[11] The Mongols then retreated from the city, encouraging those who had taken refuge in the castle to return to the town. Then they attacked again, this time using siege engines to breach the walls of the castle, killing everyone they could get their hands on.

Says Master Roger: "They perpetrated such crimes to the women that it is better to keep silent lest people get ideas for most evil deeds." The Mongols would withdraw again and people would creep out of the woods to find food in the city. But then the soldiers would suddenly return and kill those who were still alive. "And this slaughter was repeated day after day. They finally left for good only when there was no one else to kill."[12]

Taking refuge on a fortified island in the Danube also did not help Master Roger in these circumstances. The Mongols outwitted the defenders, and entered unopposed from a completely unexpected direction. He writes: "They took all the booty and left only the stripped corpses of men and women, some cut into pieces, some not."[13] Once again the Mongols feigned leaving, and returned to finish off the rest of the population.

The Mongols also seized the powerfully defended Hungarian capital of Esztergom and exacted bitter revenge on the nobles of the city who had ordered the wooden houses and suburbs surrounding the castle burned down, and with it the wealth that the Mongols had hoped to gain. Instead of taking the beautiful and handsomely dressed women for their own, as the women had hoped, they had them all robbed and beheaded. Master Roger estimates that no more than fifteen people survived the orgy of killing and burning people alive.[14]

During the spring of 1242, Ögedei Khan died, and Batu, one of the contenders for his throne, returned with his armies to Mongolia to ensure his place in the succession. Almost as quickly as they had arrived, the Mongols left Hungary, killing most of their prisoners and taking others with them. Except for several stone fortresses and castles that had held out against the Mongol assaults, Hungary had been completely devastated over the course of the year by the invasion and occupation of it lands. Easily half of its population had been killed or died during the catastrophe.

What was the killing and genocide perpetrated by the Mongols all about? Why were so many people slaughtered by the founder of the Mongol dynasty Genghis Khan and his progeny? There are no simple answers to these questions. It is surely the case that for the Mongol leaders, the killing of opponents, real or alleged, was not a matter of great concern. There seemed to be no moral code that condemned the killing of political rivals or their people. Massacre was a regular part of conquering and ruling other nations. But it was not simply a part of warfare. After belligerent peoples had been subdued, they were parceled out to individual Mongol warriors, who were given their quota to execute. The Mongols practiced extermination, in the sense that they would return to the site of mass killing and make sure they eliminated any citizens who might have survived.

It is certainly also the case that the devastation the Mongols wrought on the countryside and the tendency of the defenders to hole themselves up in castles and fortresses, as the Mongols cut them off from access to food and water sometimes for years on end, caused enormous suffering and death by starvation and disease. In the 1230s, famine and epidemic accompanied the Mongol armies as they sought to subjugate all of China. Natural disasters added to the devastation, and the Chinese population decreased by as much as one-fourth and China's development was set back for centuries.[15]

Many historians point to the deliberate and planned character of Mongol killing. In the kingdoms of Hungary and Kwarezmia, the Mongols engaged in genocide. Yet as a part of their imperial policy, the Mongols massacred large numbers of civilians wherever they went. They seemed to understand the role that terror and psychological warfare could play in destroying their enemies' ability to resist. Master Roger describes the terror felt by the surviving Hungarians, his own person included, as they were surrounded by Mongol armies and tried to find places to hide in the forest: "I already beheld my murderers in my mind's eye, my body exuded the old sweat of death. I also saw human beings, when earnestly expecting death, unable to grab weapons, raise their arms, move their steps to places of safety, or survey the land with their eyes.... I saw people half dead of fear."[16] This kind of terror made it far easier for the Mongols to conquer and to rule.

The Mongols under Genghis Khan, Ögedei Khan, and their heirs derived their power from their fighting forces and their ability to campaign in fierce and organized fashion across large stretches of territory. Eventually, infighting among the Great Khan's progeny saw the unitary empire split into political units that evolved in their own direction, depending on fortune, contingency, and location. As a result, the Mongols would never again threaten Europe or be able to command the same unified fighting machine as conquered Khwarezmia and Hungary with such force and violence.

Like the Mongols, the Crusaders were warriors on horseback, though their traditions of fighting and the weapons with which they confronted their enemies were very different from their Mongol counterparts. The Crusaders fought as soldiers of Christ, with a comprehensive medieval Roman Catholic ideology that gloried in the spilled blood of Jesus and replicated the Old Testament's sanguinary injunctions against those who would deny Jerusalem to God's people. To take the cross as a Crusader meant to express one's devotion to the pope and to obey his call for Holy War against the infidels. It also meant that if one died in the Crusade, it was an opportunity to win the remission of all one's past sins and the release of all debts or claims on one's property.

In such wars, a Crusader could rape, pillage, and kill at will, since the pope had guaranteed that there could be no sin in a campaign blessed by Christ. This also opened up the opportunity for material gain, which despite some protests against the most egregious examples, nevertheless blended easily with intense faith in the holy project of wiping out the enemies of the Lord and taking Jerusalem in his name.

Pope Urban II called for a crusade to the Near East, which became the First Crusade, in November 1095. The pope faced a number of problems. First came the appeal from the Byzantine emperor, Alexius I Comnenus, for help against the Seljuk Turks. The Seljuks had defeated the Byzantines at the Battle of Manzikert in 1071, and were advancing closer and closer to Constantinople, capturing Nicea in 1081. Then there was the pressing need of the "Reconquista" to reverse the advances of Islam and Al-Andalus, which controlled most of the Iberian Peninsula. The pope was also deeply disturbed by reports of Muslim "outrages" against pilgrims in Jerusalem and by lurid tales of Seljuk attacks against Eastern Christians in former Byzantine lands: "Wherefore, I exhort with earnest prayer—not I, but God—that as heralds of the Christ, you urge men by frequent exhortation, men of all ranks, knights as well as foot-soldiers, rich as well as poor, to hasten to exterminate this vile race from the lands of your brethren and to aid the Christians in time."[17]

Robert the Monk preached that the Mohammedans were a cruel and unclean people, "an accursed race, a race utterly alienated from God," while Baldric of Dol considered them "more execrable than the Jebusites," one of the ancient people of Canaan wiped out by the Israelites.[18] The Saracens (a generic name at the time for Middle Eastern Muslims) had delivered a piercing insult to every Christian, preached Eudes of Châteauroux. In the words of Mattathias in 1 Maccabees 2: "Alas, that I should have been born to see the ruine of my people and the ruine of the holy city! See how our holy one, our beauty and our glory is laid waste and how the gentiles have polluted her! What have we left to live for!" Like Mattathias, the preacher called his listeners to swear to Jerusalem's liberation, whatever the cost.[19] These and other Catholic clerics held out a vision of the Near East as the biblical land of "milk and honey," where life was easy and rich in comparison to the poor soil of France, where constant war was the product of shortages and poverty.

There were also concerns in Europe itself about the violence of errant knights who destroyed towns and countryside alike after the collapse of the Carolingian empire over the course of the tenth century. The popes developed the doctrine of "Peace and Trust of God" in order to persuade Christian knights to desist from internecine fighting and to heed the calls for armistice issued from Rome. But at the same time, the popes sought to find ways to convince these knights to fight against the enemies of Christendom, whether in Spain, in the Near East, or in Europe itself, where some princes of the Holy Roman Empire opposed the pope's interference in the political realm. Papal notions of holy war, in other words, came from a variety of sources at the beginning of the new millennium that linked up with the reform movement in the church.[20]

In July 1095, Urban II went to his homeland in France and, at the Council of Clermont, both denounced the violence in Europe and told stories of torture and abuse of pilgrims in the Holy Land. The reception of his call for volunteers to fight was overwhelming. Notables like Raymond IV, Count of Toulouse, and Bishop Adhémar of Le Puy joined up, as did hundreds of lesser nobles and even common folk, who took up the cause of the Crusades with a combination of great piety, the enthusiasm of the moment, and a sense of material possibilities that life in France and Europe did not offer. The so-called People's Crusade, led by the charismatic preacher Peter the Hermit, reached Constantinople months before the regular Crusader army. But due to its violent and unruly character, the mostly peasant army was forced to leave the city by Alexius II and was left to die at the hands of the Seljuk Turks. The main body of Crusader forces—some 30,000 to 35,000 fighters, including about 5,000 on horseback—similarly made its way to Constantinople, where Alexius II also quickly facilitated their exit, worried about possible disturbances regarding their need for supplies and equipment.

The Crusaders reconquered Nicea for Alexius from the Seljuks and then laid siege to the great and resplendent city of Antioch on October 20, 1097. Here, they fought for eight months before the city finally capitulated. The description of the battle scenes by Raymond D'Aguilers, canon of Notre Dame de Puy, though generously interspersed with the presence of God, nevertheless reveals the brutal character of Crusader warfare. He wrote about the taking of one of Antioch's fortifications: "With the battle and the booty won, we carried the heads of the slain to camp and stuck them on posts as grim reminders of the plight of their Turkish allies and of future woes for the besieged." This was "God's command," of course, because "the Turks had formerly disgraced us by fixing the point of the captured banner of the Blessed Mary in the ground." After the fall of Antioch (June 3), D'Aguilers wrote, the number of fallen Turks and Saracens was incalculable, "and it would be sadistic to relate the novel and varied means of death."[21]

The leaders of the Crusader armies squabbled about the fate of Antioch. In the end it was given to the possession of Bohemond of Taranto, who refused to return the city to the Byzantines and instead established a Crusader state in its environs. The rest of the Crusader armies moved south to besiege Jerusalem. On the way, Raymond IV marched into Syria and captured Albara, the first Saracen town on his route. According to D'Aguilers, "he slaughtered thousands, returned thousands more to be sold into slavery at Antioch, and freed those cowardly ones who surrendered before the fall of Albara."[22] The plunder and executions continued, while at the same time the Crusaders suffered terrible food shortages, as they encountered resistance from Seljuk and Saracen garrisons.

Cannibalism grew widespread among them, as "Christians ate with gusto many rotten Saracen bodies which they had pitched into the swamps two or three weeks before." Arguments broke out again among the Crusaders whether to advance to Jerusalem or continue the campaigns of plunder and siege of other towns. "Why shall we fight the whole world?" questioned Tancred. "Shall we kill all mankind? Think a bit; of one hundred thousand knights hardly less than one thousand remain, and of two hundred thousand armed footmen less than five thousand are left to fight. Shall we dillydally until all of us are liquidated?"[23]

Despite the many diversions along the way, usually prompted by the hope of plunder and riches, the Crusaders finally laid siege to Jerusalem.

Here, they were joined by other Crusader groups that had come to the Holy Land by sea. Even according to D'Aguilers, who tends to exaggerate their numbers, the Crusader forces were minimal: "we had not more than twelve thousand able-bodied men, along with many disabled and poor people; and as I think, no more than twelve to thirteen hundred knights." They faced, at the same time some "sixty thousand combatants in Jerusalem and women and children without number."[24]

The siege of Jerusalem was difficult and complicated, given the number of fortresses protecting the city, and the Crusaders worried about armies of reinforcements that were said to be marching from Egypt to support the defenders. The story has it that the priest Peter Dibelius had a vision in which the recently deceased bishop Adhemar instructed the Crusaders to fast and then to march in a barefoot procession around Jerusalem, much in the style of Joshua's siege of Jericho. After they did this, they breached the inner walls of Jerusalem in July 1099 and fell on the city's inhabitants, killing some Christians and Jews, along with their primary target, the Muslims.

"Some of the pagans," wrote D'Aguilers, "were mercifully beheaded, others pierced by arrows plunged from towers, and yet others tortured for a long time, were burned to death in searing flames. Piles of heads, hands, and feet lay in the houses and streets, and indeed there was a running to and fro of men and knights over the corpses." In the Temple

After laying siege to Jerusalem, the Crusaders finally conquered the city in July 1099. They then massacred the city's Muslims, as well as many Christians and Jews.
Emil Signol/Getty Images

of Solomon, he continued, using a biblical reference from John the Baptist about the Apocalypse, "crusaders rode in blood to the knees and bridles of their horses."[25] Muslim survivors of the slaughter were forced to carry the corpses outside the city, where they were piled "as high as houses" for burning.[26] When the fighting was over, Godfrey was elected king of Jerusalem, and the object of the First Crusade was won.

Within a few years of the taking of Jerusalem, the papacy sought to use the impetus for reform and unification in the church to defeat its enemies in Europe itself. The pope invoked ideas of Holy War to combat a bevy of problems, including the prevalence of simony in the church and the increasing threat of the *routiers*, bands of lawless mercenaries, who disrupted commerce, especially in the Occitane and Aquitaine in the south of France. By the 1170s and 1180s, the problem of the *routiers* overlapped with that of the perceived menace of Catharism.[27] Spreading from the south of France to northern Italy and northern Spain, the Cathars, a Manichean Christian movement, rejected the authority of the pope as that of the devil, refused to take the sacraments (including marriage), and emphasized the struggle of good and evil within the individual soul.

Local lords in the south of France tended to look positively on the Cathars, protecting the hardworking and peaceable "heretics" from papal repression, just as they often protected the *routiers* from the growing power of the king of France and his attempts to keep them from selling their services to the fractious feudal lords in the north. Particularly in the Languedoc and the surrounding region of the Occitane, the local nobles saw it to their advantage to support the independence of the Cathars and the military potential of the *routiers*. The pope was especially annoyed with Raymond VI of Toulouse for sheltering and even employing *routiers* on his lands, and for encouraging the Cathars to grow in number and prosper in his cities.

Initially, Pope Innocent III sent diplomats and preachers to win over the Cathars to the cause of the Roman Church. But unable to convince the dissenters by his arguments, the pope turned to violence. In 1204, he offered the king of France, Philip Augustus, the same indulgences given to the Crusaders in the Near East to intervene: "So that the material sword can be seen to make up for the deficiency of the spiritual sword, and you, quite apart from the temporal glory which you will earn from such pious and praiseworthy work, may obtain the same indulgence of sins which we grant to those who cross over to aid the Holy Land."[28] But the king was unwilling either to enlist himself or to allow his son Louis to lead the campaign in his stead.

In early 1208, the pope's emissary, Pierre de Castelnau, argued with the resolute Raymond VI and excommunicated him for his unwillingness to deal with the Cathars. On his way back to Rome, de Castelnau was killed, most likely by one of Raymond's knights. At this point, Innocent III called for an all-out crusade against the Cathars, the so-called Albigensian Crusade (after a major diocese, Albi, in which a large number of Cathars lived), offering all the remissions and privileges of Crusaders to the knights.

Perhaps more important as an incentive for enlisting was the pope's offer to turn over to the Crusaders the property of the Cathars and their noble defenders. This meant the possibility of gaining fiefs in the south, which the northern French nobles, backed by the king of France, were anxious to do. They donned the sign of the Cross and, under the leadership of a militant Catholic, Simon de Montfort, Earl of Leicester, and papal legate, Arnaud Amaury, Abbot of Cîteaux, assembled in Montpellier, one of the few towns in the south without a significant Cathar presence. There they were joined by groups of *routiers* who, true to their profession, were ready to sell their services to the highest bidder, despite the fact that they had been protected, along with the Cathars, by the southern barons.

While Raymond VI of Toulouse tried to placate the pope by turning over several of his best castles to him, Raymond's vassals, the Viscount Raymond Roger of Béziers, and the Counts of Foix and Comminges, were determined to resist.[29] The Crusaders then besieged Béziers, while Raymond Roger withdrew to his well-fortified town of Carcassonne. The Bishop of Béziers urged the citizens of the city to hand over 222 heretics, most of whom were heads of families, to the Crusaders in exchange for the lifting of the siege. (Some were Waldensians, a smaller, but related heretical group.) Catholic citizens were also offered the opportunity to leave the city. But in both cases, the citizens of the town refused. Like the Italian city-states, the cities of southern France harbored a fierce spirit of independence and resistance to attempts by the pope to assert his domination. The citizens of Béziers mistakenly tried to engage the Crusaders in battle, leaving the gates to the town open. As a result, the Crusaders and their *rentier* allies pushed their way into the city and engaged in one of the worst massacres in the history of medieval Europe. One of the papal legates was supposedly asked how one could differentiate the Cathars from the Catholic citizens when the killing began. His answer: "Kill them all, For God will know his own."[30] Whether he said this or not, the Crusaders killed thousands of townspeople, even dragging

Catholics from the church, men, women, and children, and slaughtering them all.

As one chronicler wrote: "Nothing could save them, neither crucifix nor altar. Women and children were killed, the clergy were killed by those crazy, damnable foot-soldiers. No one escaped; may God, if He will, receive their souls in Paradise. I do not believe that such an enormous and savage massacre ever took place before, even in the time of the Saracens."[31] It was a terrible orgy of violence; victims were blinded, tortured, and mutilated before being killed. The knights only objected when the army engaged in excessive looting. Once the inhabitants were massacred, the town was razed by fire. Satisfied with their work, the legates Milo and Arnold Amalric wrote to Pope Innocent III: "Our men spared no one, irrespective of rank, sex or age, and put to the sword almost 20,000 people. After this great slaughter the whole city was despoiled and burnt, as Divine vengeance raged marvelously."[32]

The horrors experienced by the citizens of Béziers quickly became known throughout the Languedoc. The Crusaders moved from town to town capturing and killing Cathar heretics. In Lavaur, some four hundred Cathars were burned in a single day.[33] Meanwhile noblemen who had initially resisted now turned themselves over to the Crusaders, giving up their castles and the Cathars they had protected in exchange for their lives and those of their Catholic citizens.

Raymond VI of Toulouse, who defended his retinue in Carcassonne, finally surrendered to the Crusaders in exchange for his life and that of the city's citizens. In this case, the Cathars were allowed to leave the city, while the plundering was both organized and systematic. Raymond Roger was stripped of his lands in favor of Count Simon de Montfort, and was imprisoned until his death in 1209. De Montfort himself died while besieging Toulouse to try to claim the fiefdom. Meanwhile, Raymond Roger VII of Toulouse reached a bargain with the pope, whereby he would rejoin the church and retain his lands with the promise to persecute the heretics and support the inquisition in Toulouse. Torture, terror, and execution became the fate of the Cathars and their supporters for the next half-century.

Pope Innocent was very pleased with himself. He now had a weapon with which to threaten and subdue rebellious cities. The "internal threat" to Christendom from heresy and dissenters was as important to his sense of person and attachment to power as the "external threat" from Islam in the Near East and Spain. In a letter of October 1212 to the people of Milan, the pope threatened them with the fate of the towns of the Languedoc if they continued to harbor heretics in their

The expulsion of the Cathars from Carcassonne in 1209. Although initially the city fathers were able to resist the Crusaders' advances, they eventually capitulated, expelling the doomed Cathars in exchange for their own lives. Cotton Nero E. II pt.2, f.20v, circa 1415. The British Library Board

midst: "No multitude can resist the Lord of armies: leaving aside Old Testament examples [of extermination!] just as He recently subdued the heretics in Provence" and crushed the Muslims in the victory of Las Navas de Tolosa (July 1212), "so He has the power to reduce your city to nothing."[34]

The idea of "holy war" in the Crusades contained the seeds of genocide. Christian knights were called to destroy a "vile and contemptible race" in the name of the purity of the Catholic Church as deigned by the vicar of Christ on earth, the pope. This powerful ideology blended easily with ambitions of material gain and dreams of wealth, propelling a generation of knights and retainers to undertake dangerous missions to the Near East and a series of campaigns against feudal lords of the Languedoc. The pope and his legate planned an attack on the Cathars that would eliminate them and their sympathizers from the face of the earth. A Crusade on the model of that undertaken in the Near East began that process. The Inquisition that followed finished the work of destroying a religious group, distinguishable from its neighbors primarily by its belief system. The Crusaders' marauding and killing in the Near East took on genocidal proportions but was often so indiscriminate—killing peoples of different religious groups, as in the taking of Béziers and Jerusalem—that the crimes resembled the full-scale massacres of city populations by the Mongols.

Some commentators find it difficult to classify the Mongol killing as genocide, despite its widespread and frequent occurrence. Yet the Mongols often meticulously planned their campaigns against their enemies with the clear goal of eliminating all or part of the targeted population. The Mongols wiped out en masse those groups that resisted them, even to the point of returning to destroyed cities and towns that they had targeted to finish off the survivors. True, no single group or ethnicity was identified by the Mongols for elimination. In fact, no group was exempt, though craftsmen, artisans, merchants, and builders often found a home with the Mongols. Peoples like the Hungarians, the Khwarezmians, and the Chinese were attacked with a genocidal fury that seriously reduced large population groups to fractions of their previous numbers. The attempt was to destroy the groups "as such." Unlike the Crusaders, the Mongols were not motivated by an ideology that justified destruction. Instead, killing was a method of empire building, a way to expand their territory, terrorize their opponents, and incorporate a wide variety of peoples and cultures into a vast territory stretching at some points from the Mediterranean to the Pacific. Mass killing, in some cases genocide, needed no justification. It was a fact of Mongol power and rule.

CHAPTER 3

The Spanish Conquest

The coming of the Spanish to the New World following Christopher Columbus's epic voyage of 1492 was an unmitigated disaster for the peoples of Central and South America and the Caribbean. Whatever the strengths and capabilities of the civilizations of the Americas, they were no match for the Spanish, whose combination of Catholic ideological fervor, material rapaciousness, and superior instruments of war—steel swords, armor, deadly harquebuses, and intimidating horses—brought death and destruction to the region. The peoples of the Americas were lumped by the Spanish under the name of Indians, since Columbus initially thought he had reached the fabled Indies. Among the conquistadors who followed Columbus to the region were the second cousins from the Extremadura, Hernán Cortés, who defeated the Aztecs, and Juan Pizarro, who conquered the Incas. They were adventurers, looking for riches and status, appointed by the Spanish court to undertake their respective explorations. They were accompanied by motley bands of soldiers who were no longer needed in Spain after the conclusion of the Reconquista in 1492, and by priests on a mission to convert the Indians.

The conquistadors were not Crusaders in the formal sense of the word; they received no special dispensations from the pope for their services. But their attitudes and methods were closely related to those of the popes' campaigns in the Near East and against the Cathars. Cortés, who defeated the Aztecs and conquered Mexico for Spain, carried with him an image of the Blessed Virgin and fought and conquered under the banner of the Cross, emblazoned with the Crusader slogan, *in hoc signum vinces*—"in this sign shall you conquer."[1] The conquistadors also brought with them a form of proto-racism, derived from post-Reconquista prejudice against converted Muslims and Jews.[2] The hubris of religious and racial superiority, combined with material incentives, brought about an Armageddon for the natives of the New World.

Some scholars consider the initial period of the Spanish conquest—from Columbus's first landing in the Bahamas until the middle of the sixteenth century—as marking the most egregious case of genocide in the history of mankind. The death toll may have reached some 70 million indigenous people (out of 80 million) in this period.[3] Millions of natives died of disease—smallpox, measles, influenza, and typhus, in particular—brought to the Americas by the conquest. Alien microbes traveled more quickly than did the European conquerors themselves, by the highest estimates killing an estimated 95 percent of the pre-Columbian Native American population, by the lowest estimates about a half.[4]

There is no evidence that the Spanish purposely infected the indigenous peoples. Yet the Spanish imposed conditions upon the Indians that made them more susceptible to the imported diseases. They were exploited as forced laborers and were concentrated in work camps, especially as the search for gold and silver brought a frenetic Spanish interest in mining for precious ores. The Indians were forcibly deported from their homes to alien locations for the purpose of replacing local labor of natives who had died out. The newcomers were deprived of food and water and housed, if at all, in unsanitary, makeshift dwellings. They were separated from their families and normal support systems. They were beaten, brutalized, and deprived of freedom. In his writings, Bartolomé de Las Casas, the Dominican critic of methods of the Spanish conquest, underlined the fact that the conditions of forced labor frequently led directly to the extermination of the Indians. His description of work in the mines of Hispaniola will have to stand for similar scenes all over the Spanish-held Americas.

> Both women and men were given only wild grasses to eat and other unnutritious foodstuffs. The mothers of young children promptly saw their milk dry up and their babies die; and, with the women and men separated and never seeing each other, no new children were born. The men died down in the mines from overwork and starvation, and the same was true of the women who perished. The islanders, previously so numerous, began to die out as would any nation subject to such appalling treatment.[5]

The variations on this theme of brutal mistreatment were manifold. Sometimes, the enslaved women killed their own babies and children (and sometimes themselves) because of the harsh conditions. Mining supervisors frequently raped and sexually exploited the women, with no concern whatsoever that husbands, brothers, or sons were working in the mines. Sometimes the death rates in the mines were so high that no one even bothered burying the corpses, which were instead eaten by wild animals and birds. When the Indian workers fell victim to plagues of one sort or another and eventually died, in the Franciscan Motolinía's words, "in heaps, like bedbugs," no one was there to care for them or get them food.[6] In short, the Spanish may not have purposely transmitted diseases to the indigenous peoples, but that so many perished from these diseases derived from the harsh conditions that the Spanish imposed on the Indians.

While disease may have been the biggest killer of millions of Indians who had thickly populated the Americas before Columbus's voyage, the Spanish also killed Indians in a series of genocidal episodes. The Spanish insisted on their inherent superiority as human beings over the natives. This meant they had the right to rule over them and to dispose of their lives in any way they saw fit, including eliminating them. In the words of one contemporary apologist for the destruction of the natives, the philosopher and theologian Juan Ginés de Sepúlveda: "There is as much difference between them ["these barbarians"] and the Spaniards as there is between cruel, wild peoples and the most merciful of peoples, between the most monstrously intemperate peoples and those who are temperate and moderate in their pleasures, that is to say, between apes and men."[7] Even the Aztecs, Sepúlveda continued, who claimed to have a superior culture, built cities and engaged in commerce, owned no property and lived completely at the mercy of their king, demonstrating "the servile and base spirit of these barbarians." Especially the Aztecs' religious practices, including human sacrifice, offended the Spaniards and violated their sense of decency. "War against these barbarians ["these inhumane little men"] can be justified not only on the basis of their paganism but even more so because of their abominable licentiousness, their prodigious sacrifice of human victims, the extreme harm that they inflict on innocent persons, their horrible banquets of human flesh, and the impious cult of their idols."[8] Sacrifice was unquestionably a part of Aztec religious life. The Aztecs also sometimes engaged in extreme cruelty against their enemies. But it is hard to imagine that they could have rivaled the Spanish in the sheer gratuitous quality of their brutality.

Sepúlveda ended his justification of warring against the Indians by reference to the pope's blessing of the Spanish venture in the Americas. The imperative for conversion accompanied this new breed of crusaders to the Americas. The priests who came with them seeking converts were sometimes sincere men of God who did not condone the maiming and killing of Indians occurring all around them. De Las Casas, in his lament written to Phillip II about Spanish rule in the New World, thought that these priests were too few and too influenced by the rapaciousness of the governors and military. The Spaniards treated the Indians worse than animals, he wrote, more like "piles of dung in the middle of the road. They have had as little concern for their souls as for their bodies, all the millions that have perished having gone to their deaths with no knowledge of God and without the benefit of the Sacraments."[9]

There were those priests who sought to defend converted Indians with the argument that they were now subjects of the Spanish crown and therefore could not be reduced to forced labor and slavery by the governors. The Spanish crown itself showed little enthusiasm for slavery. Columbus's efforts to turn his seizure of territories in the Caribbean into a booming slave trade for Spain were rebuked by the Crown, even to the point of imprisoning him for a short while. When Isabella tried to improve the situation for Indians by creating *encomiendas* (a system of corvée, or indentured landholding, whereby the Indian "peasants" were in theory to work the land of the Spanish four days a week and have the rest of the week to take care of their own allotments), the Spanish locals in the colonies successfully avoided any restrictions on their ability to exploit the Indians' labor and lives in any ways they wished.[10]

Isabella died in 1504, and in her will called for the Indians to be "well and justly treated." But her husband King Ferdinand maintained the Crown's right to enslave them, and, as de Las Casas noted, the treatment of the Indians only grew worse with her passing.[11] Charles V explicitly ordered the abolition of slavery among the Indians in 1530, and new laws against slavery in the Spanish colonies were promulgated in 1542. In the Papal Bull of 1537, Paul III declared that the Indians are "true men" capable "of receiving the Christian faith," and therefore should not be deprived of "their freedom and the ownership of their property."[12] Thus European ideas of how to deal with the Indians were slowly changing by the middle of the sixteenth century. At the same time, the worst of the demographic disaster had already occurred. As a consequence, the Spanish brought African slaves to the New World to do the harsh work that the Indians had previously been subjected to. Soon the numbers of Africans surpassed those of their Spanish masters. Still, the governors of the colonies and their representatives continued to condone the brutal exploitation of the Indians.

Sepúlveda conveniently left out of his treatise another characteristic of the Spanish conquest that led to the deaths of millions of natives, and that was sheer greed. De Las Casas believed that this was the central impetus behind the criminality of Spanish rule.

The reasons the Christians have murdered on such a vast scale and killed anyone and everyone in their way is purely and simply greed. They have set out to line their pockets with gold and to amass private fortunes as quickly as possible so that they can then assume a status quite at odds with that into which they were born.[13]

The Franciscan Motolinía agreed: "If anyone should ask what has been the cause of so many evils, I would answer covetousness, the desire to store in one's chest a few bars of gold for the benefit of I know not whom."[14] As gold and silver finally became accessible by taking over mines run by the Aztecs and Incas, the "insatiable greed" (de Las Casas) of the Spanish reached proportions that swept aside whatever reservations they may have had about abusing the natives. One chronicler noted about the conquerors of the Incas: "Every day they did nothing else but think about gold and silver and the riches of the Indies of Peru. They were like a man in desperation, crazy, mad, out of their minds with greed for gold and silver."[15] Against this backdrop, the lives of the Indians meant next to nothing. When Columbus first landed on the Bahamian Island of Santa Maria de la Conception (today Rum Cay) and encountered the peaceful native Lucayan tribe of Arawaks, his initial log notes for the Spanish rulers revealed a pattern of interactions that would set precedents for the century to come. His entry on Saturday, October 13, 1492, told of the small and useless trinkets that attracted the Lucayans' interest. He, on the other hand, was taken with small gold rings in Indians' noses and tried to get them to take him to the source of the precious metal, which he calculated was in the southern part of the island. He also noted the hospitality and friendliness of the natives. His entry for Sunday, October 14, 1492, stated:

These people have little knowledge of fighting, as Your Majesties will see from the seven I have had captured to take away with us so as to teach them our language and return them, unless Your Majesties' orders are that they all be taken to Spain or held captive on the island itself, for with fifty men one could keep the whole population in subjection and make them do whatever one wanted.[16]

Columbus did not come to the Indies to enslave or destroy its inhabitants. He came for gold and riches. But, in the absence of the fortune that he hoped he could discover for himself and his sovereign, Isabella II, he turned to the Indians themselves and their labor as a source of wealth. He figured he could easily conquer the Indians and use them as slaves and indentured servants in the New World or back in Spain to take care of agricultural fields, harvest crops, and labor in mines. But here, too, Columbus's plans were thwarted by the realities of the New World. The Arawaks, including the Lucayans, Taíno, and others who inhabited the islands in substantial numbers, were little suited to tasks of mobilized forced labor. The more the natives tried to escape the strictures imposed on them by the Spanish, the more brutish were the punishments inflicted on them by their overseers. The natives lived on a narrow subsistence level in pre-Columbian times. Now they had to support the new Spanish population by their work and their food gathering. Soon they began to die in very large numbers.

It is hard to know exactly how many Caribbean islanders perished in the first half-century of Spanish rule. De Las Casas claimed that the indigenous population of Hispaniola (today the Dominican Republic and Haiti) was some 3 million when the Spanish arrived, but only two hundred by the middle of the century. Cuba was totally depopulated by the forced transfer of some five hundred thousand natives to Hispaniola in order to replace the Indians who had died there. The native population of the Bahamas was essentially eliminated. The thirty or so islands in and around Puerto Rico similarly lost their indigenous population during the Spanish conquest. "All these islands," wrote de Las Casas, "are now abandoned and desolate."[17] Even taking into account some exaggeration on the part of the most prominent Spanish critic of the treatment of the Indians, it is certainly the case that both the Caribbean Taíno and Lucayans were all but wiped out in the course of the Spanish settlement.

Columbus "discovered" a number of islands after his first landing in the Bahamas. In his communications with the Spanish monarch, he praised the fertile and lush lands of Hispaniola and Cuba, and set out a vision of unusually productive agriculture manned by native slaves. He took with him back to Spain twenty Taíno captives and promised the Spanish king and queen that he would bring them such wealth that they could fund the Crusades and the taking of Jerusalem. When Columbus returned to Hispaniola in November 1493, he found that the small garrison he had left behind had been wiped out and their fortress destroyed in response to Spanish rape of local women and attacks on the Indians' property. This led to reprisals, kidnapping, and killings of locals by the Spanish soldiers.

In 1509, Spanish expeditions sailed to the islands of Puerto Rico, led by Juan Ponce de León, and to Jamaica, led by Juan de Esquivel. Much as in the five kingdoms of Hispaniola, Columbus and his henchmen murdered native elites and dragooned the peoples into forced labor in mines and on the land. Here, as elsewhere, Spanish mastiffs—terrifying fighting dogs—were set loose upon the natives, tearing many to pieces. Under Diego Velázquez, the Spanish also seized control of the heavily populated island of Cuba in 1511. De Las Casas participated as expedition chaplain and described once again the horrific cruelties inflicted on the natives by the Spanish. He wrote:

> On one occasion, when the locals had come some ten leagues out from a large settlement in order to receive us and regale us with victuals and other gifts, and had given us loaves and fishes and any other food-stuffs they could provide, the Christians were suddenly inspired by the Devil and, without the slightest provocation, butchered, before my eyes, some three thousand souls—men, women and children—as they sat there in front of us. I saw that day atrocities more terrible than any living man has ever seen nor ever thought to see.[18]

On another occasion, de Las Casas was able to save the lives of a number of local chiefs who had responded to his own entreaties to assemble and discuss their situation with the Spanish leaders. The Spanish simply wanted to burn them all to death, arguing that sooner or later they would offer resistance. Instead, they were able to flee to the hills. For those Indians who remained, the choice was either death or forced labor, and the latter turned out to be as fraught with hardships as elsewhere in the Caribbean. In Cuba, the natives routinely committed suicide as a way to avoid the Spanish depredations. "Men and women hanged themselves," wrote de Las Casas, "and even strung up their own children. Thousands died in this way." Meanwhile, by de Las Casas's count, more than seven thousand children died of hunger when their parents were taken away to work in the mines.[19]

While Columbus was an explorer and administrator, Hernán Cortés was a conquistador, who came to the New World to make his fortune and achieve fame. Starting out in Hispaniola, he participated in the invasion and domination of Cuba, along with the commander of the Spanish forces, Diego Velázquez de Cuéllar, who subsequently became governor of Cuba. Cortés quickly became an invaluable lieutenant of Velázquez's, earning a sizable *encomienda* for his services as an administrator and chief magistrate of Santiago, the island's colonial capital. Velázquez also made Cortés the commander of an expedition to explore and conquer the interior of Mexico. Cortés assembled an army of eleven ships, five hundred men, thirteen horses, and some small cannon, and made ready to depart to Mexico. But his relations with Velázquez had worsened considerably and the governor relieved him of his command. Cortés set sail with his army in any case, arriving on the coast of the

Yucatán in April 1519. There he claimed the territory, part of the larger Aztec domain of Anáhuac, for the Spanish Crown, and formally broke with Velázquez, pledging his fealty to Charles V. He scuttled his fleet off the coast of Vera Cruz, to make sure that none of his army would mutiny or try to return.

Cortés made overtures to meet with the king of the Aztecs, Moctezuma, who resided in his fabled capital, Tenochtitlán, a grand city surrounded by lakes. The Aztec king's emissaries reported back to him about the strange and powerful Spanish: with their guns ("sounding like thunder, causing people actually to swoon"), their horses ("deer that carried them ... that were as tall as the roof"), and their ferocious mastiffs ("panting, with their tongues hanging down ... eyes of coal"). Moctezuma reportedly responded with justifiable worry and fear.[20]

Getting no satisfaction from Moctezuma, Cortés proceeded inland with his army in the late summer of 1519, bolstered by recruits from the coastal tribes. His first encounters were with the Otomí people, who tried to resist his incursions. Cortés responded with the terrible violence that he had learned in Hispaniola and Cuba, attacking the Otomí and killing a substantial number. According to one native account, the Spanish "annihilated the Otomis of Tecoac, who were destroyed completely. They lanced and stabbed them, they shot them with guns, iron bolts, crossbows. Not just a few but a huge number of them were destroyed."[21] He then marched south to Tlaxcala, which had been in conflict with Moctezuma and opposed his imperial ambitions. The Tlaxcalans also resisted Spanish overlordship. Cortés attacked again, dispersing the Tlaxcalan army. He proceeded to burn towns and villages, killing men, women, and children, who scattered before his horsemen.[22] Cortés then sent representatives to the Tlaxcalan chiefs, threatening them with complete elimination—"within two days we should go and kill them all and destroy their country"—if they did not submit and join his campaign against Moctezuma.[23] The Tlaxcalans agreed to his terms and sent some five thousand Indians to join the campaign.

Only the powerful city of Cholula stood between Cortés and Tenochtitlán. Cortés tricked the Cholulan leaders into gathering in an assembly room to talk. As he wrote to the Spanish king:

> I sent for some of the chiefs of the city, saying that I wished to speak with them. I put them in a room and meanwhile warned our men to be prepared, when a harquebus was fired, to fall on the many Indians who were outside our quarters and on those who were inside. And so it was done.[24]

The city of Cholula was the only major barrier between Cortés and the Aztec capital of Tenochtitlán. Under the guise of carrying out negotiations, Cortés and allied Tlaxacalans entered the city and slaughtered as many as ten thousand Cholulans. Félix Parra, Episodes of the Conquest: The Massacre of Cholula, *1877. D. R. Museo Nacional de Arte/Instituto Nacional de Bellas Artes y Literatura, México*

A terrible slaughter ensued. Deprived of their leaders, the Cholulans stood no chance against the Spanish, who burned down houses and buildings and massacred the population of the city. Cortés wrote to the king: "We fought so hard that in two hours more than three thousand men were killed."[25] The Tlaxacalans, no friends to the Cholulans, continued the massacre along with the Spanish. Some women and children were spared and fled to the hills. The Spaniards, wrote Cortés's secretary, "were dripping with blood and walked over nothing but dead bodies."[26] Thousands, maybe as many as ten thousand, Cholulans were killed.[27]

By the time Cortés crossed over the mountains to Tenochtitlán, he had assembled a large army of Spanish and Indian recruits. Moctezuma allowed Cortés and the Spanish to enter the city, as a way to discern their intentions and weaknesses and seize them if the need arose. But Cortés, fearing problems, moved first, surprising Moctezuma and taking him prisoner within his palace, from which the Spanish ruled the city. The Spanish were duly impressed by the beauty and sophistication of Tenochtitlán—the emperor's zoological collection was a particular favorite—but this did not keep them from accumulating a stash of gold and precious stones through their control of the emperor, whose passivity in these circumstances has puzzled observers ever since.[28] In Cortés's absence from the capital, one of his deputies, Pedro de Alvarado, massacred a group of Aztec nobility during a religious ceremony, which he apparently interpreted as a threat to the Spanish. Cortés hastened back to Tenochtitlán, but it was too late. The massacre set off a local rebellion; a crowd of angry citizens killed Moctezuma, who was blamed for the murder of their nobles, and Cortés had to withdraw from the city to plan his next move.

That came in January 1521 when Cortés besieged Tenochtitlán, destroying the surrounding towns in the process. The Spanish built bridges over the lakes and attacked the city. Once again, the Spanish and their Indian allies were ruthless in their assault, slaughtering some six thousand residents of the lakeside town of Ixtapalapa, before entering the city itself and laying waste to its population. Cortés hanged the new emperor Cuauhtémoc and the rulers allied with him, while the Aztec priests were "given to the dogs." The surviving young women and boys were seized and branded as slaves.[29] The men were put to work for Cortés, rebuilding the city—now Mexico City—for the Spanish. Cortés ordered the burning of books and records of the Aztec empire and the monuments that spoke of its greatness. He also destroyed the idols in the temples and had the edifices cleaned and purged of the remnants of sacrifices in order to prepare them as places of worship for Catholics.

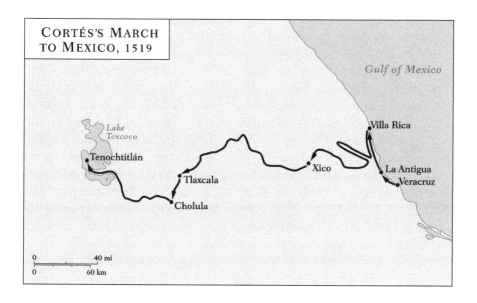

CORTÉS'S MARCH
TO MEXICO, 1519

Gulf of Mexico

Lake Texcoco

Tenochtitlán

Villa Rica

Xico

Tlaxcala

La Antigua

Veracruz

Cholula

0   40 mi
0   60 km

The conqueror of the Aztecs writes: "Considering that Tenoxtitlán had been so great and so famous, we decided to settle in it.... If in the past it was the capital and the queen of all these provinces, it will be so, the same, henceforward."[30]

King Charles appointed Cortés governor of "New Spain of the Ocean Sea," and the conquistador proceeded to develop his territory by opening mines, supporting agriculture, and starting the first sugar plantation in the New World. He also spread the *encomienda* system throughout his realm, forcibly indenturing large numbers of Indians to the estates, while enslaving others to work in the mines. Indicative of the genocide perpetrated in Mexico, after Cortés and the Spanish took over the realm of Moctezuma in the period 1519–21, the population fell by as much as 85 percent, to as low as 1 million in 1600.[31]

There was a close linkage between Cortés's conquest of Mexico and the Spanish incursions into Guatemala in terms of the personnel involved and the violent methods they brought with them. The major difference was that the Mayan kingdoms that ruled most of today's Guatemala, both the highlands and the coastal regions, were bitter rivals, and there was no central capital to capture, like Moctezuma's Tenochtitlán. Pedro de Alvarado, who had led the slaughter of the Aztec noblemen in Cortés's absence from Tenochtitlán, was sent in 1523 by the Mexican governor to conquer the lands to the south. Alvarado led an army of some five hundred Spanish soldiers, plus large contingents of Tlaxcalan and Cholulan allies. De Las Casas accused Alvarado of carrying out what he called a "holocaust" against the Mayan peoples of Guatemala, and certainly the imagery fits Alvarado's campaigns.[32]

The campaign against the Incas in Peru conducted by Cortés's distant cousin, Francisco Pizarro, highlights the intimidating technological superiority of the Spanish forces over the much more numerous indigenous population. In this case, the Spanish attacked the large and well-developed Inca empire, headed by King Atahualpa, who was both a secular ruler and a deity to his people. Self-consciously modeling his tactics after those of Cortés and inflamed by the rumors of gold and riches in the land of the Incas, Pizarro launched two brief campaigns in Peru in 1524 and 1526 before getting the approval of the Spanish king to launch a third in 1530. Accompanied by his brothers, Hernando and Pedro, and the conquistador Hernando de Soto, Pizarro marched inland in the direction of the Inca city of Cajamarca, where Atahualpa, his retinue, and his army were resting at a nearby hot springs. Pizarro sent emissaries to Atahualpa demanding that he submit to the king of Spain, but Atahualpa indignantly refused to do so. The confrontation between Pizarro and the Incas at Cajamarca is well known because of a number of surviving accounts by the Spanish, including those of Pizarro's brothers.[33]

Pizarro tortured some local Indians in order to find out Atahualpa's whereabouts at the nearby hot springs. The conquistador's tiny army of sixty-two cavalrymen on horseback and 106 infantrymen marched to Cajamarca, where they were dazzled and frightened by the sight of an Inca army of anywhere between forty thousand and eighty thousand warriors, encamped in the foothills behind the city. When representatives of Atahualpa came to greet the Spanish, Pizarro invited the king to meet with him in his camp, promising that "no harm or insult will befall him." Pizarro then planned an ambush, concealing his cavalry and infantry, and setting up his meager cannon to strike the center of the large plaza where he hoped to entice the king. The ruse worked; clearly the Incan monarch did not expect such a small force to try to overwhelm him, especially since he came with several thousand unarmed warriors and nobles, adorned in their finest garb. Atahualpa himself "was very richly dressed, with his crown on his head and a collar of large emeralds around his neck." He was transported on a splendorous gold-bedecked litter carried by eighty of the leading nobles of the land, while other high chiefs were also carried in litters and hammocks accompanied by "squadrons of Indians with crowns of gold and silver."

Pizarro entreated the Dominican friar Vicente de Valverde to convince Atahualpa to submit to "the law of our Lord Jesus Christ and to the service of His Majesty the King of Spain." The friar approached the Incan monarch with a cross in one hand and the Bible in the other, explaining to Atahualpa that all of this was ordained in God's book. There are several versions of what happened next. But all agree that the king looked at the book and threw it to the ground in disgust. The priest was outraged by this blasphemy, denouncing the Inca king and calling to the governor: "March out against him, for I absolve you!" Accompanied by the blowing of bugles, Pizarro's cannon fired at the huge crowd of Indians in the square. The Spanish horsemen charged into the mass of humanity with swords and lances; rattles were hung from the horses, which apparently made a terrible racket, frightening the Indians even more. "The Indians were so filled with fear," wrote one reporter, "that they climbed on top of one another, formed mounts, and suffocated each other." Since the Incas were unarmed, Pizarro's troops were able to kill almost all of them. The nobles who carried Atahualpa's litter were cut to pieces by the Spanish soldiers, but they stood their ground, even without their limbs. When they fell other nobles took their place. Finally, a number of Spanish horsemen were able to knock the king's litter to the ground and Pizarro captured Atahualpa alive. The slaughter did not let up until nightfall as the Spanish pursued those who tried to escape, making sure to kill all the nobles. Some seven thousand Incas died in the battle, "and many more had their arms cut off and other wounds." All of those who were transported in the litters or who carried them were killed.

Pizarro explained the horrible massacre of November 16, 1532, to the captured King Atahualpa as the inevitable consequence of God's will: "By reason of our good mission, God, the Creator of heaven and earth and of all things in them, permits this, in order that you may know Him and come out from the bestial and diabolical life that you lead." The Indians would appreciate in the end why it was "good that we have done you" by coming to their land and conquering them in the name of the king of Spain. Of course, Pizarro's invocation of God and king could not conceal his monstrous greed. He demanded of Atahualpa that he purchase his life by filling a room twenty-two, by seventeen, by nine feet, with precious gems, gold, and silver. Once the king had managed to accumulate this huge treasure, Pizarro had him executed on trumped-up charges on July 26, 1533.

During the months between the slaughter of Cajamarca and the execution of the king, Pizarro gathered more Spanish troops in his camp and found allies among the Indians to help him conquer the capital of the Inca empire, Cuzco, which he did later in 1533. The Spanish were stunned by the beauty and refinement of the city, but that did not prevent them from plundering it and tearing apart precious Inca works for the gold and silver encased in them. Once Cuzco was conquered, all the former Inca lands fell into the hands of the Spanish. Especially in the mines of Potosí, which are now in Bolivia, the Spanish found what they came for—a rich and deep source of silver, one which eventually flooded the European continent with Spanish wealth. Of course, this came at the expense of the native population, which was forced to work in the mines in fearsome conditions. As a later Spanish visitor noted (1638): "Every peso coin minted in Potosí has cost the life of ten Indians."[34]

Some assert that because the Spanish crown did not intend to wipe out the Indians of the Caribbean, Mexico, or South America, the killing of the native population by the conquistadors and the high mortality from the diseases spread by the Spanish cannot be considered genocide.[35] This argument is often supported by the outcome of the

Valladolid disputation of 1550–51, when the church rejected the notions of Sepúlveda that the Indians deserved to be enslaved and deprived of their property. If Columbus, Cortés, and Pizarro killed in the name of the king and the Cross, they did so, the church now concluded, without the mandate of either.

Yet the conquistadors operated in a framework that was created by the Spanish Crown. Their readiness to kill at will and to wipe out entire towns and villages, slaying men, women, and children, derived from their pathological state of mind when confronting the native inhabitants of the New World. They were far away from home and thus from any constraints that their own society might force them to observe. There were virtually no Spanish women who accompanied them to the New World. So they routinely seized wives and daughters of chiefs and kings to be their mistresses. Still they looked down on the indigenous peoples of the Americas and considered them their inferiors, whose lives meant nothing and whose blood could be shed without any hesitation or moral qualms. They admired the cities built by the Incas and Aztecs, even noting that they were in some ways superior to their own at home in Spain. But that did not seem to rub off on their views of the Indians themselves, whom they found to be despicable and not worth keeping alive unless under slavery.

The way they tortured and killed the Indians reflected a deep-seated hostility to their victims' very existence as human beings. Part of this came from their understanding of the meaning of the Catholic Church and the alien character of those who were not part of its covenant. They were their own kind of crusaders, though they had no Jerusalem to liberate. The conquistadors hacked and burned their way through the Americas, killing at will and with unimaginable cruelty, revealing the mentality of genocidaires, ready to eliminate whole towns and villages, tribes and peoples, in order to attain the land and wealth of the New World. They were "governors," empowered by the Spanish Crown to rule in its name and by their priests to murder the supposed savages who refused the Cross. The killing was in the name of a better Spanish and Catholic world for the Indians, since the one they possessed did not matter in the least to the conquistadors.

CHAPTER 4

Settler Genocides

The establishment of overseas empires began with the Spanish and Portuguese explorations of the New World and Africa in the sixteenth and seventeenth centuries, and expanded to encompass the globe with the emergence of British, French, and later German and Italian claims, from the late seventeenth century until the First World War. With overseas empires came colonies, and with colonies came settlers. The conquistadors and their armies were the purveyors of genocide in the New World. Many of them continued in their new role as governors of their respective colonial territories. Settlers soon followed. Attacks on the indigenous populations of Spanish America did not stop. But already the indigenous peoples of Central and South America had been reduced to a small percentage of their numbers on the eve of Columbus's first voyage.

In those territories taken over by the British and French—North America, the Antipodes (Australia and New Zealand), and Africa—incidences of genocide more often followed rather than predated the influx of settlers. The colonial powers were ultimately responsible for genocide, and therefore sometimes this phenomenon is known as colonial genocide. Settler genocide makes more sense here to indicate that armed civilians, organized militias and posses, carried out the bulk of the killing. Sometimes the imperial governments at home were not involved at all, or even opposed the attacks on the indigenous peoples. Sometimes these depredations took place without overseas expansion, in continental expanses like the United States or Imperial Russia, which can be considered in some ways to have colonized themselves.

Scholars have pointed out the deep paradox in a situation in which the new European arrivals attacked and sometimes eliminated the indigenous peoples as interlopers. European settlers purveyed an entire ideological system whereby they were the natural heirs to the land of the indigenous peoples, and those peoples, whether Aborigines in Australia, native peoples in North America, or Bantu tribes in South Africa, were the aliens. This ideology was buttressed by ideas of race, where inferior "small and dark" peoples, itinerant and ignorant, had no right to the land, even if they were to claim it in any formal way, which they often did not.

Part of this ideological system predated the arrival of the settlers and had its origins in seventeenth-century British ideas of property, by which the land belonged to those who tilled the soil and harvested crops, built homes and fences, and created wealth from the soil. But the major source of conflict came not from ideology but from the violent confrontation between European pastoral settlers—those who herded cattle and sheep, though marking out territory as their own—and the indigenous hunter-gatherers, whose patterns of living from and with their natural surroundings sometimes dated back thousands of years. In its most unadulterated form, this was a conflict about land. The settlers wanted land to graze their animals, while the indigenous peoples needed it for collecting berries, roots, and grubs; hunting animals, large and small; and providing a full panoply of social needs, from medicinal herbs to religious icons.

The most violent of these confrontations took place with the emergence of the modern age, meaning with the French Revolution, the Industrial Revolution, and the development of the nation-state at the end of the eighteenth and beginning of the nineteenth centuries.[1] The accompanying rapid growth of urban centers in Europe led to increasing demand for wool (for textiles) and meat (for consumption) that in turn attracted fresh waves of settlers to the American West, Australia, and South Africa. New sources of mineral wealth in all these places also attracted settlers and prompted urban growth, which stimulated demand for the products of ranchers and farmers. The open lands of the hunter-gatherers were increasingly encroached upon, sharpening tensions and prompting outright warfare, though almost everywhere of an asymmetrical character. The sheer distance from the metropolitan centers and the relatively underdeveloped character of local government meant, more often than not, that settlers "took the law into their own hands," prompting massacres and genocide.

The authorities acted with increasing resolution to protect the settlers from the resistance of the indigenous populations. The state also sometimes sought to protect the indigenous populations from the settlers, but did so in a way that made few concessions to the unique economic and cultural needs of the peoples involved. Native peoples were forced onto reservations of one sort or another "for their own protection," limiting—if not eliminating—their ability to hunt, gather foodstuffs, and husband the land as they had done for centuries. The state forcibly placed their children in schools, sometimes even removing them from their families and cultures in the process. The sense of the inevitability of the end of "primitive" civilizations among the leaders of government served as a self-fulfilling prophecy, one political leaders encouraged by their own actions, whatever their humanitarian intentions might have been.

The victory of the American colonists over their British rulers in the War of Independence near the end of the eighteenth century raised new dangers for the survival of the indigenous American Indian tribes. But it also spelled hard times for the Australian Aborigines. In search of new outlets for their growing population, both free and convict, the British formally established their first colony in the Antipodes, New South Wales, in 1788. Although the French also made some efforts to explore Australia during the same period, the British—perhaps through their North American experience—understood the importance of transporting colonists to establish a foothold in the new land mass. Magnificent harbors and rich land in Australia gave the British the confidence to send shiploads of both convicts and freemen to develop their new territories.

The indigenous aboriginal tribes that lived in Australia and engaged in a variety of hunting and gathering occupations did not stand a chance against the new settlers, especially since the latter were backed by military units and armed militias. Although the British insisted that they meant no harm to the Aborigines and intended to protect their rights, the inherent conflicts between stock farmers, in particular, and the Aborigines soon led to violent resistance. In what became a familiar pattern in most settlements in the coastal regions of Australia, the Aborigines stole and slaughtered livestock of the interlopers to protect their lands, while the settlers engaged in massacres against the Aborigines. From the pre-colonization population of some 1 million Aborigines, only 31,000 survived by 1911, a devastating reduction of 97 percent.[2]

The British island colony of Van Diemen's Land (renamed Tasmania in 1856) was established on June 14, 1825, though settlers had been living and working there, often as sealers on the surrounding islands, since the late eighteenth century. Modest trading networks between the sealers and the Aborigines led to a situation in which some aboriginal women lived among the sealers and became surrogate wives and laborers. A small population of Creoles gradually grew up around the sealing settlements and spread to the island as a whole. About 150 miles from the mainland, separated by the Bass Strait, the island became

The expanding farming and sheep and cattle industries in Australia put pressure on traditional aboriginal hunting grounds starting in the early 1830s. In response, Aborigines began to attack white settlers more resolutely, leading to the military campaigns by local authorities and murderous settler posses to destroy aboriginal communities. National Library of Australia/MS 1234; vn1234567; MUS Nm785. 3054 S437; ORAL TRC 1030/1

increasingly attractive as a British outpost because of its European climate, ample rainfall, and rich pastures. The British founded the first successful settlement of Van Diemen's Land, the town of Hobart, in 1804, and from 1812 until mid-century, the British sent shiploads of convicts, overwhelmingly men, to inhabit the island and serve the needs of its free settlers.

Much as the sealers established a stable relationship with the Aborigine population—sometimes more brutal in their exploitation of the indigenous peoples, sometimes less—so did the first settlers and the convict laborers live in relative harmony with the Aborigines in the early days of the island's colonization. There was enough land and resources to go around, and the newcomers did not substantially threaten the livelihood of the Aborigines. During this period, the Aborigines were generally known to be gentle, sweet, welcoming, and unthreatening souls, even if one discounts the inevitable idealization of the "noble savage" that underlay many contemporary accounts. There were some six to eight thousand Aborigines living in Tasmania at the outset of British colonization in 1800, though there was already some decline in the population as the result of exposure to previously unknown diseases. The Aborigines were divided roughly into five "nations" and lived in what were called "Settled Districts" in the eastern part of the island.[3] Escaped convicts and itinerant roustabouts periodically hunted the Aborigines as if they were wild animals, taking their women for their own malicious pleasures. The welcoming and gentle disposition of the Aborigines quickly began to change.[4]

Even more important to the development of the colony was the huge growth in the sheepherding economy—what Australians called the wool industry—prompted both by the natural gifts of the island's grazing lands and by the British 1822 tariff act, which greatly reduced the costs of importing Australian wool. By 1851, sheep-farming districts in Australia produced half of Britain's needs for raw wool in the textile mills of northern England.[5] Between 1816 and 1823, the number of sheep in Tasmania quadrupled to 200,000; by 1830, the number was 682,000; and in 1836, it was 911,000. In that same period, the European population increased from 2,000, roughly the same as the population of Aborigines, to 23,500.[6]

Relations between the settlers and the Aborigines notably worsened in the early 1820s, as the colony was established and the growing herds of sheep began to impinge on the Aborigines' hunting grounds. Henry Melville, a pioneer Tasmanian newspaperman, described these rapidly changing relations between the colonists and the natives and the attempts of the local government to deal with the problem:

> In this year [1824], the aborigines of the Island began to annoy the settlers to a degree that required some active measures of the Government to allay the outraged feelings of this ill-fated race of human beings. These poor bewildered creatures had been treated *worse* than were any of the American tribes by the Spaniards. Easy, quiet, good-natured, and well-disposed towards the white population, they could no longer brook the treatment they received from the invaders of their country. Their hunting grounds were taken from them and they themselves were driven like trespassers from the favorite spots for which their ancestors had bled, and had claimed by conquest.... The stock-keepers may be considered as the destroyers of nearly the whole of the aborigines—the proper, the legitimate owners of the soil; these miscreants so imposed upon their docility, that at length they thought little or nothing of destroying the men for the sake of carrying to their huts the females of the tribes; and, if it were possible in a work like this to record but a tithe of the murders committed on those poor harmless creatures, it would make the reader's blood run cold at the bare recital. In self-defense were these poor harmless creatures driven to

desperate means, their fine kangaroo grounds were taken from them, and thus were they in want of their customary food; and when every other means of obtaining a livelihood was debarred to them, *necessity* compelled them to seek food of their despoilers.[7]

Melville went on to explain that the lieutenant-governor in charge of the island, Colonel George Arthur, was generally well disposed to the Aborigines, as was Melville himself. But there was really no way of controlling the situation. "The evil was far too rooted," Melville wrote, and that it had become "*a war to the knife*," in which the Aborigines killed settlers if they could, while the settlers proceeded to wipe out the Aborigines in systematic fashion. "This murderous warfare," writes Melville, "in the course of a few years destroyed thousands of the aborigines whilst only a few score of the European population was sacrificed."[8] What Melville does not tell us is that Arthur himself, though opposed to the unseemly killing of the Aborigines, was primarily responsible for the development of Tasmania into a sheepherding dynamo. He built roads, supported landowners, and profited greatly himself from the growth of the island's wool industry and from his own landholdings. His historical reputation is also called into question by his close association with the influential landowner Roderic O'Connor, who had advocated arming convict bounty hunters, urging them to finish off the surviving natives.[9]

Lieutenant-governor Arthur's inability to bring to an end the ongoing conflict between the settlers and the Aborigines, labeled the "Black War," led him to call for military actions against the Big River and Oyster Bay nations, which had refused to vacate their territories on his demand. Between November 1826 and April 1828, some four hundred Aborigines were killed in a series of attacks and massacres. The situation became particularly acute when the Aborigines responded to the abduction and murder of two of their women in October 1828 by doing the same to three white women.[10] This was the ultimate indignity for Arthur, and he promptly declared martial law on the island and labeled the Big River and Oyster Bay peoples "open enemies of the state."[11] He subsequently launched a carefully mapped-out military campaign to drive all of the Aborigines into the Tasman peninsula in the south-eastern corner of the island, isolated from the white community and its economic activities. The idea, widely circulated among the Tasmanian landowners and townspeople, was to cleanse permanently the towns and grasslands of Van Diemen's Land of "the blacks." The *Launceston Advertiser* wrote: "Really it is high time they were either removed out of the Island or driven by force of arms to the uninhabited districts."[12]

This would please the stockholders, since they would have free run of the island for their herds and flocks. Lieutenant-governor Arthur imagined, as did many good Victorian progressives, that such a measure would also provide the Aborigines with the opportunity to acculturate peacefully to British norms and ways of life.

In the fall of 1830, Arthur came up with the plan of crisscrossing the Settled Districts, about a hundred miles of territory, with a series of intersecting armed lines of men to catch the remaining free Aborigines in his "net." Enacted by more than two thousand soldiers, settlers, and convicts—almost every able-bodied man on the island—the idea was to drive the Aborigines from their traditional lands in the eastern part of the island to the Tasman peninsula. But the elaborately developed net caught only four Aborigines, two of whom were killed and two captured. The failure was accentuated by the fact that four British soldiers were accidently killed in the campaign. But the entire effort intimidated the indigenous tribes to the extent that they eventually agreed to leave their land for Flinders Island in the Bass Strait.

By this point, only about two hundred Aborigines had survived the Black Wars and the various diseases that had been spread among them by the colonists. The prevalence of syphilis among Aborigine women, initially contracted from the settlers and convicts, had radically decreased the fertility rates among the indigenous population. The killing, the spread of disease, and the deprivation had taken a severe toll on the Aborigine population. On Flinders Island, the Aborigines had to endure the religious and cultural instruction of the earnest Presbyterian pastor George Augustus Robinson, and began to die out as a result of the miserable conditions in which they were forced to live. By the late 1840s, only forty-seven Aborigines were still alive. Flinders was abandoned in 1847 and the survivors were taken to Oyster Cove, not far from Hobart on the Tasmanian mainland. The last full-blooded Tasmanian, known as Truganini, died in 1876.[13] Although some of the offspring of the sealers and aboriginal women, and other Creoles, continue today to identify with their aboriginal roots, the languages and cultures of the native Tasmanian peoples were essentially eliminated.

Though divided into distinct groups, as were their cousins on the Australian mainland, the Tasmanian Aborigines could be considered a separate ethno-national unit that was slated for elimination by the settlers, supported and sometimes initiated by the local government, and were therefore victims of genocide. They were killed by disease and by the deprivation brought on by colonial settlement. But they were also massacred in large numbers over a period of several decades. There were thirty-seven confirmed massacres between 1823 and 1834 alone, with a minimum of six and a maximum of forty Aborigines killed in each. In total, 870 were killed on the orders of the Van Diemen's Land government, roughly half of them in a massacre.[14] Most of the massacres took place at aboriginal camps at night or at dawn. The perpetrators were armed soldiers, convicts, policemen, and settlers. Sometimes, there was "cause," like the murder of a stockman or a shepherd, and sometimes there was simply an opportunity to kill blacks. The end result was the same: the elimination of the Tasmanian Aborigines.

The fate of North American Indian tribes frequently resembled that of the Australian Aborigines. European settlers arrived on their native territories and claimed the land for their own. When the Indians resisted, the settlers, supported by their colonial governments, or their national, state, and local governments, were quick to drive out or kill the Indians and their families or to force them onto reservations to live out their lives in alien surroundings. As in the case of the Aborigines, children were taken from Indian families, women were kidnapped and raped, promises of peace were made and broken, and claims of racial and civilizational superiority were used by the settlers to justify their land grabbing and their killing. North American native peoples, like the Aborigines, were highly susceptible to the diseases brought to their homelands by the settlers and prone to the abuse of alcohol, which the settlers purposely employed to undermine their ability to resist. Those settlers who raised livestock, primarily cows and sheep, tended to have the sharpest conflicts with the Indians, provoking massacres and outright warfare between Indian tribes and government and militia formations. The tendency of the North American settlers to see the Indians as hopelessly primitive and incapable of marshaling the resources of the land gave them "reason" to deprive those Indians of the most desirable lands and territories.

It is difficult to apply the appellation "genocide" to the entire experience of Aborigines in Australia. Certainly genocide fits the history of the Tasmanian Aborigines, as well as, no doubt, of those of Victoria and Queensland. Other Australian Aborigine groups were subjected to discrimination, pressure on land, exploitation, and episodes of forced assimilation, but not necessarily genocide. Similar issues of differentiating the various experiences of genocide from those of other forms of criminal discrimination, murder, and oppression exist when thinking about the North American tribes. Although the Indians, like the Aborigines, faced consistent racism, exploitation, and land grabs on the part of the settler population, they were not all victims of genocide.[15]

One of the first documented cases of mass murder of North American Indians was the destruction of the 3,000 to 4,000 Pequot in New England during the period 1637 to 1640. In one terrible 1637 attack, "the Pequot were utterly destroyed, to the number of six or seven Hundred," wrote a participant, Captain John Mason from Connecticut, using Old Testament images: "There were only seven taken captive and about seven escaped.... Thus was God seen in the Mount, ... burning them up in the fire of his Wrath, and dunging the Ground with their Flesh." Subsequent attacks included massacres of the men, the enslavement of Pequot women and children, deportation to the Caribbean and other colonies, and forced assimilation to other tribes. The Connecticut Assembly proclaimed "that the river that used to be called the Pequot shall be called the Thames, and the place called Pequot should no longer be so called, but its named changed to New London."[16]

Two centuries later, the "removal" of the Cherokees from Georgia in 1838 and their forced march on the "Trail of Tears"—an "eight hundred mile nightmare"—across the southern states to a reservation in Arkansas cannot be considered genocide, even though a substantial number of Cherokees, as many as 8,000 out of 18,000, died as a result of internment, disease, exposure, and hunger.[17] Here, the historical terminology of "ethnic cleansing"—violently driving out a people from their territory without the goal of elimination—can most fruitfully be applied. The unhappy fate of the Comanche, Apache, and Sioux, among others, who famously resisted the incursions of the "white man" and wreaked considerable havoc on the settlers and their families in the Great Plains and the Southwest before being defeated and sometimes massacred by the Army and confined to reservations, reflects the general pattern of settler genocide, though does not contain the crucial element of intentionality with the goal of elimination.

The extermination of the Yuki Indians of California's Round Valley near Mendocino constitutes yet another story of the violent confrontation of settlers and native peoples. This relatively small tribe of 7,000 to 11,000 members on the eve of the settler influx in the late 1850s was wiped out between 1856 and 1864. Genocidal killing and forced confinement to the reservation reduced the number of Yuki to 85 males and 215 women.[18] The numbers continued to decline in the late nineteenth century as a result of starvation and sickness, as well as episodic fights with the settlers. The Round Valley Reservation still exists as the home of some 100 Yuki, plus a number of other California tribes. There are a handful of Yuki speakers still alive.[19]

An old Yuki woman in mourning photographed by Edward S. Curtis in 1924. In the early 1850s, before being attacked by settlers and rangers, around 10,000 Yukis lived in California; today, only about 100 Yuki still live on the Round Valley reservation. Edward S. Curtis Collection/Library of Congress LC-USZ62-11580

The Yuki were a hunter-gatherer tribe who lived off of the roots, berries, acorns, clover, wild vegetables, and herbs that grew plentifully in Round Valley (sometimes known as Nome Cult Valley), some two hundred miles north of San Francisco. The Indians also hunted deer and birds and fished for salmon and trout. Round Valley, noted a contemporaneous report, "is a beautiful plain, circular in form, containing about twenty-five hundred acres of land nearly all of which is susceptible of a high state of cultivation, lying among the mountains in the north-eastern part of Mendocino County, and capable of sustaining, under judicious management, about twenty-five thousand Indians."[20] The coming of the settlers changed all that.

On February 2, 1848, the Treaty of Guadalupe Hidalgo was signed, ending the Mexican-American War and ceding California to the United States. Almost at the same time, on January 24, 1848, gold was discovered at Sutter's Mill in Coloma, in the Sierra foothills. The gold rush that followed brought some 300,000 people to California, both from the East Coast of the United States and from abroad. While the prospectors fanned out into the foothills, many of the newcomers settled in the boomtown of San Francisco. The city required much more food and housing, and local ranchers and settlers looked for new lands to graze their animals. Round Valley served as a perfect destination for the herdsmen, causing immediate conflicts with the Yuki, Round Valley's inhabitants. The settlers and their herds of cows and horses trampled the traditional products of Yuki foraging. Indians were attacked and beaten by the settlers, who thought of them as "savages" at best and little more than animals at worse. The Yuki began to retaliate by killing the settlers' cattle for food and driving off their horses.

California was admitted to the Union as a state in 1850, and its new government decided to set aside a reservation in 1856 for the Yuki in the northern part of the valley as a way to avoid confrontation between the settlers and the Indians. Some 3,000 Indians moved to the reservation, while others scattered around the valley and into the woods to the north and east, merging, in some cases, with other tribes that lived in the region.[21] For their sustenance, the Indians would return to the valley to hunt game or gather roots and acorns, only to be driven off by the settlers, who were increasingly aggressive in shooting the Yuki and kidnapping their women for sexual exploitation. As the settlers claimed property and fenced off their ranches, they also set out in posses to punish the Yuki for rustling. In response, the Yuki sometimes killed whites, though in much smaller numbers than their own losses.

One of the settlers, Dryden Laycock, provided a brief history of the killing to an 1860 investigatory committee of the California Senate:

> In one thousand eight hundred and fifty-six the first expedition by the whites against the Indians was made, and have continued ever since; these expeditions were formed by gathering together a few white men whenever the Indians committed depredations [usually the theft of stock]; there were so many of these expeditions that I cannot recollect the number; the result was that we would kill, on an average, fifty or sixty Indians on a trip, and take some prisoners, which we always took to the reserve, frequently we would have to turn out two or three times a week.[22]

The situation on the reservation was no better than for those Yuki who lived scattered in the hillsides and around the valley. The government agents on the reservation could not stop the settlers from using the reservation's grazing lands as their own. The Yuki were poorly supplied, and malnutrition and hunger grew more acute among them. The spread of diseases of various sorts, including venereal disease, killed some Indians and weakened many others. The settlers continually raided the Indians on and off the reservation, raping women, killing the men, and kidnapping many children. Unarmed except for bows and arrows, the Yuki were no match for the posses. According to a contemporaneous newspaper report, in a series of raids, syphilis-infected settlers raped some five or six hundred "squaws" of the nearby Clear Lake Indians—"not a solitary individual was exempt—dooming the entire tribe to extinction."[23] Yuki children were frequently abducted as semi-slaves and servants, since the forcible indenturing of Indians was legal until 1863. As a result, one Indian reservation agent, Vincent Geiger, reported in 1857: "the Indians ... have very few children, most of them doubtless having been stolen or sold."[24] Scattered Yuki retaliation to settler raiding only enraged the settlers more, and some called for the elimination of all the Yuki. The Indians' theft of a single stallion resulted in the massacre of 240 Yuki. A farmer claimed he lost twenty hogs and shot three Indians and four others were hanged at the reservation for the crime.[25]

The Round Valley Wars turned overtly genocidal in 1859, when the governor of California, John Weller, authorized the formation of the so-called Eel River Rangers, headed up by the settler and noted "Indian killer" William S. Jarboe. Jarboe and his band of vigilantes had already been responsible for the murder of some sixty-three Yuki men, women, and children.[26] He was then authorized by the governor to deal with the problem. His way of doing it, as he told his rangers, was: "Kill all the bucks they could find, and take the women and children prisoners."[27] For Jarboe and his men, the Indians were less than human; they were vermin, who stole and concealed, hid and ran, not at all worthy opponents of the settlers. Some three hundred Indians were killed in Jarboe's campaign; another three hundred were sent to the reservation. For his work, Jarboe presented a bill to the state of California for $11,143.[28]

The state government's investigation of the Mendocino wars revealed attitudes toward the Yuki that were shared by settlers and their representatives when faced by Yuki opposition to their encroachments. There were many who found the killings justified as the only way to deal with the "thieving and murderous" Yuki. Even those who did not like the killings found it hard to consider the Yuki as equals. *The Majority Report* notes, for example, that one should not "dignify, by the term 'war,' the slaughter of beings, *who at least possess the human form* and who make no resistance and make no attacks, either on the person or the residence of the citizen."[29] "I do not consider them as hostile," testified George W. Jeffress, who also maintained the innocence of the Yuki, "but rather as a cowardly thieving set of vagabonds: I do not consider that they are brave when two white men can drive twenty-five of them, and shoot them down while they are running."[30] The government investigation of the Mendocino war concluded: "History teaches us that the inevitable destiny of the red man is total extermination or isolation from the deadly and corrupting influences of civilization."[31] The majority of the committee clearly advocated that the Indians should be protected on the reservation and kept separate from the settlers. The problem was that they counted on the federal government to help them do this, but the Army was reluctant to intervene. The *San Francisco Bulletin* reported, for example: "The United States troops located in that region [Mendocino] are represented to be pursuing, during all these troubles, a 'masterly course of inactivity.' "[32] Some Army units were even stationed on the reservation. But they could not stop the incessant raiding against Indian villages, and did not have the ability to pursue the criminals outside the reservation borders.[33] As a result, the periodic raids on the reservation continued as the Yuki died in large numbers from hunger and disease. As the Army officer in charge, Captain Johnson noted: "I believe it to be the settled determination of many of the inhabitants [settlers] to exterminate the Indians." There was "no way of preventing it."[34]

Settler genocide also took place in European colonies in Africa. The San people, known earlier by the derogatory appellation Bushmen, from the Dutch "Bosjesman" and the later Afrikaans "Boesman," wandered over a good part of southern Africa before the arrival of the Dutch East India Company in 1652. Company representatives built and manned a small station at Table Bay for restocking their ships. As part of their effort to ensure a fresh supply of meat and vegetables, the company invited Dutch settlers to farm the lands in the immediate vicinity of what became Kaapstad, or Cape Town. The settlers—some Huguenots and German Protestants were also involved—were encouraged to move to South Africa by the offer of free passage, cheap land, mostly on rental terms, and the initial capital to set up a homestead. Because of the scarcity of water and good grazing lands, the settlers, who became known as trekboers, moved from place to place, increasingly impinging on the territories of the San and of the Khoikhoi, a Bantu-speaking people, themselves mostly pastoralists.

Although their numbers were not huge—it is estimated that there were about six hundred independent stockholders scattered through the western Cape in 1770, out of a total Dutch population in the Cape of about 15,000—the trekboers roamed over a very large expanse of territory, and their herds and their own hunting patterns soon became a serious challenge to both the San and the Khoikhoi.[35] The trekboers overwhelmed the Khoikhoi and increasingly integrated them into their own economy as herders, servants, and employees. The San resisted, initially episodically, then in a more violent and determined manner. Sometimes the Khoikhoi joined the San in their efforts to keep the trekboers from taking over their traditional lands. Complicating matters was the fact that there were no hard-and-fast distinctions between the San and Khoikhoi, who were sometimes simply identified as Khoisan.

We have very few documents that illuminate the thinking of the San as they faced the incursions of the trekboers. But the stubborn ferocity of their resistance, like that of the Yuki and the Aborigines, offers some insight into their mentality. The trekboers' herds trampled fields where the San women gathered roots, bulbs, and other natural vegetables, and destroyed the grazing land that fed the wild animals, mostly gazelles and ostrich, that the San hunted and ate. The trekboers themselves hunted, sometimes simply for amusement, depleting the San's supply of game for food and other animal products. The trekboers made biltong, a jerky (brined, salted, or smoked), out of eland, which became very popular in settler communities as well as in Kaapstad, meaning that the herds of this crucial animal in the San diet, as well as spiritual life, rapidly diminished.[36] The San fighters were angry, relentless, and even mocking of the trekboers, as they insisted on their sovereignty over the land and threatened the settlers. They used forms of guerilla warfare to attack the trekboers and their settlements, slaughtering animals, setting houses on fire, and sometimes killing settlers themselves. They rustled cattle and poisoned trekboer waterholes. One traveler cited a farmer who said "when he went out in the morning [he] found near his house his whole herd, consisting of forty oxen and two hundred sheep, several dogs and horses, and some Hottentots [Khoikhoi] who were employed to guard them all murdered, not a single one having escaped."[37]

The response of the trekboers was predictable. Initially, represent-atives of the Dutch East India Company led parties of settlers organ-ized into "commandos" into the back country to attack and destroy groups of San. Over time, the administrators of the Cape Colony had other preoccupations and left the punitive expeditions to the settlers themselves. By the end of the eighteenth century, these commando raids were annual affairs, with as many as 250 trekboers on horseback, along with their allies, including their Khoikhoi herders, heading out to kill the San. Sometimes, more informal commandos were raised to track down alleged San offenders. As in the case of attacks on Aborigines or American Indians, these attacks usually came at dawn, as the raiding parties found the campfires of the San and assaulted them at daybreak, usually killing all the men and taking women and children as prisoners. The women would serve in trekboer agriculture and do menial tasks around their homesteads. Sometimes they were "given" to the Khoikhoi help as wives. The San children were indentured to the trekboer families in what amounted to slavery, except they could not be sold or bought, and were in theory free of their obligations once they reached adult-hood. But it is also true that the trekboer raiding parties often killed women and children in quite horrible ways. Cases were reported of San women's breasts being used to make tobacco pouches. Children's skulls were bashed against rocks. In one August 1775 case, a trekboer commando killed a number of hippopotamuses and left them along a riverbank as an ostensible gift to the San. When the natives came to feast on the gift of fresh meat, the trekboers ambushed them, killing 122 and taking 21 prisoners.[38]

The killing of San became routine among the trekboers, who considered the San, as one local official noted, as "not actually human, but at the same time he cannot really be classified among the animals. He is, therefore, a sort of creature not known elsewhere."[39] One traveler, writing in 1775, observed that the trekboers often hunted the San as if they were game. "Does a colonist at any time get sight of a Bushman, he takes fire immediately, and spirits up his horse and dogs, in order to hunt him with more ardour and fury than he would a wolf or any other wild beast."[40] The racist colonists bragged to each other about the number of San they had shot, as if, wrote another observer, they had been speaking about partridges.[41] From virtually every perspective, the San people became the objects of trekboer aggression: as pagans among Christians, as blacks among whites, as hunter-gatherers among farmers and ranchers, as "primitives" among the civilized. The result was to slate the San for extinction. If, at the beginning of the commando actions, the talk was about killing those San who had engaged in hostile activities, by the end of the nineteenth century, the Council of Policy agreed to the killing of the San whenever and wherever they could be found, essentially the sanctioning of genocide.[42]

It is impossible to know how many of the 30,000 Cape San were still alive when the British first seized the Dutch East India Company colony in 1795 and then again permanently in 1806, as a way to keep the territory out of the hands of their French rivals. But it is reasonable to conclude that not more than a third remained. The methods of British rule were far different from those of the Dutch. The British had abolished slavery in their empire and professed a humanitarian and missionary zeal for absorbing the remaining San into Cape society. In the name of protecting the San people and defusing the tensions between the settlers and the hunter-gatherers, the British created a reserve for the San in the north, known as Bushmanland. They also supported efforts to Christianize the San population by establishing missionary stations on the frontier. The British governor, George Macartney, also tried to foster a program of convincing the trekboers to donate goats, sheep, and cattle to the San as a way of getting the natives to engage in a settled pastoral existence. He wished to "impress them with a sense of the benefits arising from permanent property, preferable to casual and predatory supplies."[43] Yet the diminution of the number of the San continued. Unofficial trekboer commandos continued to attack and destroy San encampments. The British even authorized some commando raids in response to San rustling of cattle or other attempts to defend their territory.

The missionary stations shut down one after another, as the San showed little interest in "converting" to Christianity and instead used the stations as a way to seek relief from raiding commandos and from periodic drought and famine. The program to encourage the San to turn into pastoralists by giving them their own herds of animals came to little, as more often than not, the hungry San slaughtered the animals and shared any excess meat with their fellow tribesmen.[44] Bushmanland was semi-arid and the San found it difficult to support their traditional way of life. But even at that, the Cape Colony government could not protect the San from the incursions of the trekboers, who were constantly looking for fresh "unclaimed" pastureland. The growing trekboer population also put pressure on those lands that were supposedly set out for the San. New methods of boring holes for wells made it possible for the trekboers to support their herds in Bushmanland and in other semi-arid lands where the San had been able to live isolated from the trekboers. When Merino sheep were introduced into the Cape Colony in the 1850s, roughly at the same time that these highly adaptable animals transformed the landscape of Tasmania, Bushmanland became the home of the constantly growing trekboer herds. To make matters worse for the San, pressure grew from the north, as the Griqua people began to attack and kill the San, ostensibly for raiding their herds. Suggestions by reformers for setting up sanctuaries for the San within Bushmanland received little support from the government.

By mid-century, it had become increasingly difficult for independent groups of San hunter-gatherers to support their way of life in Bushmanland, as well as anywhere else in the Cape Colony. The same stereotypes plagued the San that were there from the beginning of the confrontation with the settlers. The *Standard and Mail* wrote in 1873: "He neither plows nor sows, he does not rear cattle or sheep, he is in truth a wild animal in human shape, preying on whatever he can lay his hands on, now stealing sheep now grubbing up roots, now feeding on mere garbage when nothing else comes his way."[45] With little compunction, the trekboers and Griqua (and sometimes other pastoralist tribes) killed the San on sight. They also died from hunger, with the shortages of game and traditional foods caused by the growth of the trekboers' herds. And they died from thirst, as they were driven farther into the most arid portions of the already dry Bushmanland. The frontier to the east also provided no succor for the San. The only way they could survive was to offer to work for the trekboers—herding, some farming, carrying firewood, and so on—in exchange for a bit of food, implements, and blankets. As had been common on the frontier since the arrival of the trekboers, there was bartering in San children, though the practice was formally abolished by the British.

In their desperation, the San would combine their scavenging existence with working for the trekboers. With their women and children often attached to the trekboer households, the men had little choice but to live in a form of bondage. Alcohol and disease became an everyday part of their lives. As the San gradually were drawn away from their hunter-gather lives, their distinctiveness as a people also dissipated. Those who survived became a kind of underclass of "coloreds" in South African society, while isolated bands managed to roam the Kalahari Desert until the twentieth century. Of the original Cape San, only about thirty "unhybridized" members remain.[46] The San population of South Africa today is, however, much larger, given the immigration of San from southern Angola and Namibia.

The Cape San were the victims of genocide. The Dutch East India Company and its trekboer compatriots engaged in a murderous elimination of San hunter-gatherers who had resisted their incursions into traditional San territories. Although the policies of the British were less directly genocidal, they nevertheless also contributed to the killing of the San people and forced them deeper into territory where survival became increasingly precarious. Meanwhile, the Cape Colony's policies of assimilating San tended to sink them deeper into misery, with many dying of disease, hunger, and the deprivations caused by menial labor on trekboer farms. The Cape San, as a people and a way of life, could not survive.

Modern Genocides

There are many aspects of modernity that encouraged some of the worst characteristics of genocide. The shrinking of the world, celebrated in Jules Verne's *Around the World in Eighty Days* (1873), meant that military forces could be transported quickly and efficiently to locations at home or abroad when modern state leaderships determined that threats by supposedly alien peoples should be crushed. Modern communications—telegraph, teletype, and telephone—made it possible for genocidal orders to be transmitted instantaneously over long distances. The development of modern iron, steel, and machine-building industries encouraged rapid innovations in weapons technology. New means of killing became available to political elites that sought the elimination of enemy peoples in warfare and genocide. The influence of modern media on politics and governments made it possible for extremist political parties to spread their messages of hate and destruction to an ever larger number of people dispersed over large expanses of territory. Modern politics itself, which involves the competition of political parties for the allegiance of masses of people, created situations in which ethnic and religious minorities and other "undesirable" groups could be isolated, slated for "removal," or even eliminated. The modern state also facilitated these processes through its inherent need to count, keep track of, and order its population. The all-seeing state had little tolerance for anomalies or alternative identities among its subject peoples.[1]

The maturation of modern nation-states at the end of the nineteenth century overlapped with the emergence of integral nationalism, a new and more virulent form of political thought that essentialized racial and ethnic differences between peoples. With deep portents for the future, this kind of pseudo-scientific political thinking asserted that biologically defined nations were locked in a Darwinian struggle for supremacy. This was, as one formulation put it, "when nationalism began to hate."[2] A number of scholars have noted the important relationship between the racialist violence of settler genocide and the subsequent development of violent state ideologies and practices on the continent.[3] The settler genocide described in the previous chapter was superseded by a new and more dangerous form of mass killing that harnessed the power of the modern state to its murderous ends. In some ways, the last notable settler genocide of the pre-World War I colonial era—the killing of the Herero and Nama in German South West Africa—can also be considered the first genocide of the modern period, as the German state and the German army became directly involved, and the interests of the settlers themselves were a relatively minor part of the story of mass murder.

The Germans were relative latecomers to the scramble for colonial possessions. They came to South West Africa, now Namibia, only in the mid-1880s. Through a combination of deal making with the pastoralist and mostly sedentary Herero and Nama (sometimes known as Namaqua) tribes, they were able to carve out territory for German settlers. Unlike the Cape San, the Herero and Nama had firmly entrenched chiefs, who could bargain with the Germans as a way to control the pace and extent of the colonialists' entry into tribal territories. Unfortunately for the Herero and Nama, the Germans were no different from other imperial powers in the unreliability of their promises and the readiness of their settlers to claim more land and resources than they were allotted, especially when it was at the expense of the "inferior" black natives of the region.

The Germans were anxious to develop their colony in South West Africa as a way to demonstrate their power and commitment to their imperial rivals, the British and French. They soon hatched plans for an east–west railroad that would divide the Herero lands into two, and as rumored, to place the natives on reservations. The Herero herdsmen also found themselves increasingly in debt to German traders, which exacerbated relations between the local government, led by the relatively progressive governor of South West Africa, Col. Theodor Leutwein, and the Herero. As a way to ease the tensions, Leutwein called for the payment of all debts and the squaring of accounts, which was impossible given the absence of a money economy among the Herero. When the traders began to seize Herero cattle as payment, the Herero chief, Samuel Maharero, instigated a revolt against the Germans in January 1904. In calling his men to arms against the Germans, Maharero was careful to instruct them not to kill German women or children, missionaries, or British and Boer inhabitants. In the initial fighting, some 120 to 150 Germans were killed (some Boers, as well).

Governor Leutwein was in no position to control the Herero uprising with his limited armed contingents, so he turned to the German
imperial government for assistance. The German General Staff, backed
by the Kaiser, was insistent on showing firmness in dealing with the
rebels, sending General Lothar von Trotha to South West Africa in June
1904 with fourteen thousand regular troops. Leutwein and von Trotha
did not at all see eye to eye about how to deal with the natives. The
governor hoped that the presence of German soldiers would coax the
Herero into coming to terms with the colonial government and sign a
treaty. Von Trotha, schooled in the German military tradition of bring-
ing opponents to their knees by destroying their fighters and leveling
their society, sought to eliminate the Herero altogether.[4]

The biggest confrontation with the Herero came at the Battle of
Waterberg, August 11–12, 1904, where von Trotha's troops defeated
some three to five thousand Herero combatants, leaving the only possible avenue of escape through the desert to the east. This was anticipated by a study made by the German General Staff of the prospective
war. "If, however, the Hereros were to break through, such an outcome of the battle could only be even more desirable in the eyes of the
German Command because the enemy would seal his own fate, being
doomed to die of thirst in the arid sandveld."[5] Von Trotha's infamous
Schrecklichkeit (horror) order to the Hereros called for genocide: all the
Herero men would be killed and the women and children shot at and
driven out.

> I, the great general of the German soldiers, send this letter to the Herero
> people. Hereros are no longer German subjects. They have murdered,
> stolen, cut off the ears and noses and other body parts from wounded
> soldiers, and now out of cowardice refuse to fight. I say to the peo-
> ple: anyone delivering a captain to one of my stations as a prisoner
> will receive one thousand marks; whoever brings in Samuel Maherero
> will receive five thousand marks. The Herero people must leave this
> land. If they do not, I will force them to do so by using the great gun
> [artillery]. Within the German border every male Herero, armed or
> unarmed, with or without cattle, will be shot to death. I will no longer
> receive women or children but will drive them back to their people or
> have them shot at. These are my words to the Herero people.[6]

At the same time, he let his troops know that it would not be good
to kill all the women and children, as it would sully the reputation of
the German army. As the bedraggled Herero retreated farther into the
desert, they grew increasingly hungry and thirsty. When the Germans
caught up with them, the Herero were immediately killed, including

many women and children. The chief, Maharero, managed to cross the Kalahari Desert into Bechuanaland along with about a thousand Herero, and found refuge by swearing allegiance to a local chief. The remaining Herero in the colony were set upon by German soldiers and attacked, shot, and hanged. Von Trotha then turned his attention to the smaller Nama people, whom he threatened with the same fate of dying of hunger or being killed by the Germans: "Those [Nama] ... who refuse to surrender will have happen to them what happened to the Herero people, who in their blindness also believed they could successfully make war on the mighty German Kaiser and the great German people."[7]

Leutwein was beside himself at what he considered the irrational and immoral killing of innocent Hereros who, he argued, could and should be used as labor in the colony. His viewpoint finally won support back in Berlin; von Trotha was recalled in November 1905, and rewarded with a number of military decorations. But the policy of incarcerating, rather than killing, the Herero ended up destroying them

Seven Herero men held captive in German South West Africa during the Herero rebellion in 1904–6. Although captured women and children sometimes were allowed to live, generally the Germans killed the men and boys even after they surrendered. Chronicle/Alamy Stock Photo

through imprisonment and forced labor. The labor camp set up at Shark Island—some seventeen hundred Herero and Nama expired there by April 1907—turned out to be a death camp, with roughly 80 percent of those who were sent there never returning. Twelve to fourteen prisoners died every day. They were poorly fed, exposed to nasty weather, beaten with the notorious sjambok (a heavy leather whip), and sent out as slave labor to private firms.

The atrocities in South West Africa were described in a series of interviews with returning transport workers that appeared in the South African *Cape Argus* newspaper. Afrikaners and Englishmen expressed their shock at the killing and sjamboking of women and children. In the September 25, 1905, issue, one young Afrikaner stated that the Germans killed twenty-five women and children in February 1905, mostly "strung up to trees by the neck and then shot." He continued:

> The Germans said they were spies, but they were captured with the natives with whom we had been fighting and some of the children could not have been older than five. A lieutenant gave the orders. Five soldiers would take each woman or child in turn, put a rope round their neck, string them up over a branch and then shoot them. No, the women did not shriek for mercy. They never said a word. They were glad to be released from their suffering, for they had been very cruelly treated. The children were quiet, too, as a rule. Like the women they had had an inch of bayonet into them time after time, as well as being badly treated in other ways.[8]

Between 1904 and 1907, the Herero were reduced from some 80,000 robust cattle herders and their families to 15,000 or so hungry and disease-prone refugees, driven off their land by the Germans and isolated in labor camps. Von Trotha's policies reflected a particularly homicidal version of policies of military repression. Von Trotha himself had been active in crushing native resistance in German East Africa in the period 1894–97 and in suppressing the Boxer Rebellion in China in 1900. His racist proclivities, combined with the idea that nothing less than the complete destruction of the Herero and Nama peoples would quell the uprising, led directly to genocide.

Although the site of the Armenian genocide, in the late Ottoman Empire, was thousands of miles away from German South West Africa, and the circumstances of the mass killing very different, there were some interesting and important linkages between the two. Most notably the German army and state were implicated in both.[9] For example, German army officers were directly involved in some of the Ottoman Turkish actions against the Armenians, most prominently in advising the Ottoman Turkish authorities about how to deal with the Van Uprising of April–May 1915. It is important to add, however, that the Germans were not perpetrators in the case of the Armenian genocide, even if German army and diplomatic representatives knew about the persecution and killing of the Armenians and did little or nothing to stop either.

As in the settler genocide, there were notable elements of competition over land and wealth between the Turks and Kurds, on the one hand, and the Armenians, on the other, that played a role in the developing conflict. Recent Muslim refugees from the Balkans and the Russian Empire—known as the muhajirs—also looked with considerable avarice on the Armenian holdings and, later on, frequently took possession of their property after the removal of Armenian families. During the deportations themselves, the muhajirs often treated the Armenians with particular callousness and brutality.

The elimination of the Armenians from Anatolia depended on a specific confluence of international and internal factors. The outbreak

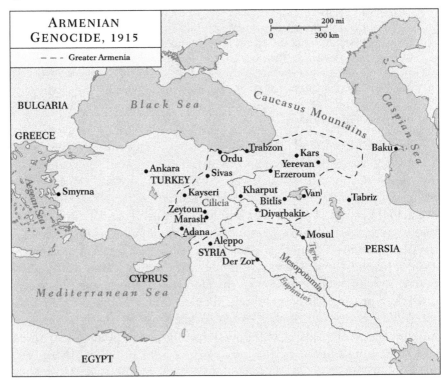

Most Armenians in the Ottoman Empire lived in compact communities in eastern Anatolia. During the Armenian Genocide of 1915, those who were not murdered immediately—mostly women, children, and the elderly—were driven from their homes through the desert in the south to Der Zor and beyond the Euphrates River. Over a million Armenians perished as a result.

of World War I was critical to the genocide, in that the Ottoman Turkish government could undertake its actions against the Armenians under the cover of wartime security measures. It also mattered that the diplomatic history of the prewar period played out in such a way that the Ottomans were allied with the Central Powers (Germany and the Habsburg Empire), and not with the Entente (Britain, France, and Russia). That the Armenians were the targets of the Turkish authorities in the first place derived, at least in part, from the fact that the Armenians had been the object of international concern, especially on the part of the Russians, British, and French. In the Treaty of Berlin (1878), the Allies imposed on the Ottomans Article 61, which obliged them to protect the Armenian population. Just prior to the outbreak of World War I, on appeals from the Armenian leadership, the Allies pressured the Ottomans to sign the "The Armenian Reform Agreement" of February 8, 1914, which compelled the Young Turk government to accept the presence of international inspectors in Ottoman territory, who were to look out for Armenian interests. Turkish officials considered these agreements a sign of betrayal on the part of the Armenians and an insult to Ottoman dignity and sovereignty.[10]

The Armenians had also been the target of Ottoman Turkish pogroms during the long reign of Abdul Hamid II (1876–1909), known as "the Red" for his allegedly blood-thirsty disposition. There were terrible massacres of Armenians in Sassoun, Trabzon, Zeytoun, and elsewhere between 1894 and 1896. Some 200,000 Armenians were killed or wounded in these rampages, which were supported by irregular Ottoman Kurdish troops, the so-called Hamidians. Periodic killings of the Armenians continued to take place until the outbreak of World War I. The worst episode took place in the province of Adana in 1909, where some 20,000 Armenians were slaughtered during riots by hungry and homeless migrant workers and Islamic discontents, supported by the local Ottoman officials.[11] The centuries-old millet system, whereby the major religious groupings (Armenians, Jews, Greek Orthodox) within the Ottoman Empire enjoyed a modicum of security and autonomy within their communities while relegated to subordinate status to Muslims, began to break apart by the middle of the nineteenth century. Islamic assertions of superiority over the Christian communities took on violent manifestations.

Although most Young Turk and Armenian political leaders were of one mind during the Young Turk Revolution in 1908 in seeking a modern, constitutional government for the Ottoman Empire, the Young Turks' intellectual evolution from the founding in 1906 of their political party, the Committee of Union and Progress, and the Ottoman entry into

World War I in October 1914 took on increasingly Turkish ethno-nationalist and anti-Armenian dimensions.[12] Once the Ottoman Empire entered the war on the side of the Germans and Austrians, the Armenians' general sympathies with the Russians and with Great Britain and France rankled the Young Turk leadership. To make matters worse, the direct threat of a Russian invasion from the east produced the specter of collaboration in the heavily Armenian populated region around Lake Van in eastern Anatolia. Although there was little evidence that the Ottoman Armenians would actively take part in a Russian assault, the Young Turks used the Russian offensive and episodic Armenian collaboration as a pretext for deporting all of the empire's Armenians. The only exceptions were the Armenians in the cosmopolitan cities of Constantinople, Smyrna, and Aleppo, who had extensive contacts with Western merchants and diplomatic representatives.

The beginning of the Armenian genocide is traditionally dated from the night of April 24, 1915, when a group of some 250 leaders of the Armenian community of Constantinople were arrested and sent into exile, the majority of them executed in the process. Meanwhile, Armenian soldiers who had been in the Ottoman army were removed from their normal units, disarmed, and sent to work in labor brigades. Many of these soldiers were also eventually executed. The genocidal process was accelerated by the Armenian uprising in Van in April and May 1915. As reports came into the city from around the countryside that Armenians were being disarmed and deported from their homes, the Van Armenians decided to resist. Although the uprising was eventually put down by the Turkish army, advised by the German General Liman von Sanders, and the Van Armenians were deported like all the rest, the Turkish government took umbrage at their resistance and proceeded with increasing brutality to deport the remaining Anatolian Armenians.[13]

Typically, the Young Turks communicated orders to local Ottoman officials, sometimes reinforced by members of the "Special Organization," to disarm and deport "their" Armenians. The "Special Organization" was made up of a motley group of former criminals, fervent nationalists, policemen, muhajirs, and pure adventurers, who used their power over the Armenians, and sometimes over local officials, to wreak havoc on their victims, torturing, extorting, and exploiting Armenian men and women in the most base ways. When the Armenians were notified in advance of their impending deportations, they frequently rushed to sell their property at cut-rate prices, in the hope of accumulating enough cash to survive the coming ordeal. But once under way, they were robbed, not just of their money but also often of their means of transportation, their food supplies, and even their clothes. The men were usually taken off separately and shot in remote locations. Women and children, the elderly, and the infirm were then sent on forced marches over the burning sands of the Mesopotamian desert and across the Euphrates River in the south. Their guards tormented them and gave them no succor.

Without food, water, and protection from the elements, several hundreds of thousands of Armenians died in the process of the deportation itself. Many went mad wandering naked in the desert; some threw themselves and their children into the Euphrates. The Ottoman Turks also knew that sending the Armenians to specific destinations in the south, Der Zor being the best-known example, would result in their death, since there were simply no resources to support additional inhabitants.[14]

The sheer brutality of the Armenian atrocities was seared into the memory of the men and women who survived them. One such survivor, an Armenian cleric, Grigoris Balakian, described numerous instances of people trapped by their killers and slaughtered—the appropriate verb—in the most horrible ways. He learned much from the Turkish commander of his caravan, Captain Shukri, who told him about the massacre of the Yozgat Armenians, who had been separated into groups of men and of women and children. "Did you shoot them dead or bayonet them?" Balakian asked Shukri:

> "It's wartime, and bullets are expensive. So people grabbed whatever they could from their villages—axes, hatchets, scythes, sickles, clubs, hoes, pickaxes, shovels—and they did the killing accordingly." It is impossible for me to convey what happened to those 6,400 defenseless women, virgins, and brides, as well as children and suckling infants. Their heartrending cries and doleful pleas brought down the deaf canopies of heaven. The police soldiers in Yozgat and Boghazliyan who accompanied us would even boast to some of us about how they had committed tortures and decapitations, cut off and chopped up body parts with axes and how they had dismembered suckling infants and children by pulling apart their legs, or dashing them on rocks. Oh, it is useless to try to depict such carnage.[15]

Although the Young Turks attempted to conceal the worst aspects of the deportations and genocide, there were too many Western observers in the empire to keep the horrors hidden from international attention. Especially, missionaries and diplomatic representatives could see the suffering of the Armenians with their own eyes. Henry Morgenthau,

Armenians were burnt alive in Sheykhalan (in the province of Mush) by Turkish soldiers. This photo was taken by Russian soldiers in eastern Anatolia in 1915. Armenian Genocide Museum Institute

the American ambassador to the Ottoman government, collected these reports and left an unforgettable account of the fate of the Armenians:

> The ferocity of the gendarmes apparently increased as the journey lengthened, for they seemed almost to resent the fact that part of their charges continued to live. Frequently any one who dropped on the road was bayoneted on the spot. The Armenians began to die by hundreds from hunger and thirst. Even when they came to rivers, the gendarmes, merely to torment them, would sometimes not let them drink. The hot sun of the desert burned their scantily clothed bodies, and their bare feet, treading the hot sand of the desert, became so sore that thousands fell and died or were killed where they lay. Thus, in a few days, what had been a procession of normal human beings became a stumbling horde of dust-covered skeletons, ravenously looking for scraps of food, eating any offal that came their way, crazed by the hideous sights that filled every hour of their existence, sick with all the diseases that accompany such hardships and privations, but still prodded on and on by the whips and clubs and bayonets of their executioners.[16]

Morgenthau estimated that somewhere between 600,000 and 1 million Armenians died in this exodus. The numbers are probably higher, though Morgenthau had a remarkable grasp of the realities on the ground at the time.

Equally important to Morgenthau's understanding of the deportation of the Armenians were his interviews with Talât Pasha, the leading member of the "triumvirate" of Young Turk rulers. After one such discussion with Talât, stated Morgenthau, citing his diary of August 3: "He gave me the impression that [he] Talât is the one who desired to crush the poor Armenians." Talât also told Morgenthau that the deportation of the Armenians was an official policy that had been adopted after considerable discussion. During another interview, Talât decided to reveal to Morgenthau the "reasons" for the deportations:

> In the first place, they [the Armenians] have enriched themselves at the expense of the Turks. In the second place, they are determined to domineer over us and to establish a separate state. In the third place, they have openly encouraged our enemies.... We have therefore come to the irrevocable decision that we shall make them powerless before this war is ended.

Morgenthau protested that none of these charges made sense. "It is no use for you to argue," Talât responded, "we have already disposed of three quarters of the Armenians; there are none at all left in Bitlis, Van, and Erzeroum. The hatred between the Turks and the Armenians is now so intense that we have got to finish with them. It we don't, they will plan their revenge." Therefore, he continued, "We will not have the Armenians anywhere in Anatolia. They can live in the desert but nowhere else." Morgenthau concluded that Talât genuinely despised the Armenians as a group, and wanted them eliminated. To a plea from Morgenthau regarding a particular Armenian, who was a friend of the Ottoman government, Talât responded: "No Armenian can be our friend after what we have done to them."[17]

The Armenian genocide did not have a clear and definable conclusion. Many tens of thousands of Armenians continued to die of hunger, disease, and exposure in 1916, as the survivors of the deportations sought to stay alive on meager supplies in encampments and temporary quarters in towns like Der Zor and Ra's al-'Ayn in the south. Some Armenians managed to make their way to Lebanon and Egypt, where they found relief for themselves and their families. In November 1919, when the French took over the occupation of Cilicia from the British, some Armenians returned to their homes, in the hopes of reestablishing themselves in their native lands under Allied protection. With difficulty, they sought to reclaim Armenian women and girls, who had converted to Islam and allowed themselves be taken into Turkish and Kurdish harems to save themselves from impending privations and death. When Mustafa Kemal (Atatürk) led a successful campaign of the Turkish armies to reestablish Turkish control of Anatolia in 1921–22, the returning Armenians either fled for their lives or were driven out by the authorities of the new Turkish Republic. Many thousands of Armenians also died in the borderlands of eastern Anatolia, where they were caught between the hostile Turks and the Russian Civil War in the period 1917–1918.

Not unlike the Armenians, the Assyrian Orthodox population of southeastern Anatolia, a territory straddling the present-day borders of Turkey, Syria, Iraq, and Iran, was subjected to the genocidal policies of the Young Turk government. Meanwhile, the Pontic Greeks, who lived on the shores of the Black Sea, suffered through a series of deportations, pogroms, and massacres in the period 1916–1922, which took some 300,000 to 350,000 lives.[18] At the conclusion of the Greek-Turkish war in 1922, the Aegean Greeks were ethnically cleansed from Anatolia and, according to the provisions of the Treaty of Lausanne of 1923, the remaining Orthodox Greeks were exchanged with the Muslim (mostly Turkish) population of Greece.

The Nazis were well aware of the Armenian genocide and of the general indifference of the world to the fate of the Armenians. Talât Pasha, who took refuge in Germany after World War I, was assassinated on the streets of Berlin in 1921 by the Armenian nationalist and genocide survivor Soghomon Tehlirian. In a well-publicized trial, the court pronounced Tehlirian innocent because of "temporary insanity" brought on by the suffering of his people. Shortly before the Nazi invasion of Poland, Hitler is known to have said to his assembled generals on August 22, 1939: "Our war aim is not to attain a particular line [in the east], but the physical destruction of an enemy.... Who after all speaks today about the annihilation of the Armenians?"[19] This was in connection with his injunction to the Wehrmacht to destroy the Polish nation without mercy in the coming conflict.

Virulent anti-Semitism was integral to Nazi ideology from the very beginning. Hitler's infamous book *Mein Kampf*, which has to be considered the "bible" of the National Socialists, was permeated by accusations against the Jews for undermining the health of the German people, stealing their wealth, and subjecting them to the dire goals of a Jewish world conspiracy, sometimes directed from Moscow, since Jews were the heart and soul of communism, and sometimes from Wall Street, since Jews were also intent on controlling world capitalism. Hitler's portrayal of the struggle with world Jewry was based on an apocalyptic, pseudo-religious vision of his own mission: "I believe I am acting in accordance with the wishes of the Almighty Creator: *by defending myself against the Jews, I am fighting for the work of the Lord.*"[20] Hitler also blamed the Jews for the "stab in the back" that cost the Germans the humiliating defeat in World War I and unjust treatment at the Versailles Peace Conference. The Jews were the root cause of the economic and political woes of the Weimar Republic, which became especially severe at the end of the 1920s and beginning of the 1930s, with the onset of the Great Depression. The soulless, stateless Jews even posed a biological threat to the German nation, because their very "race" carried the detritus of subhumanity. Miscegenation spelled doom for Germans and Germany.[21]

Hitler came to power in 1933 in good measure because of promises to pull Germany out of its social and economic crises. The Nazis promised to create jobs for the German people in a period of severe unemployment brought on by the Great Depression. They promised stability, when strikes and street battles characterized the life of the big cities and industrial centers. For Hitler and the Nazis, the "plague of the Jews" was inseparable from Germany's myriad problems. The message of virulent anti-Semitism seemed to strike home to millions of Germans, though certainly not all. For those members of the elite German business, financial, and military establishments who sided with Hitler and allowed him to assume the chancellorship, his anti-Jewish ranting may have seemed like a small and insignificant part of his platform. Few Germans could have imagined in 1933 the level of destructiveness and horror that Hitler's anti-Semitic designs would bring to their country and the world.

Hitler's "road to genocide" was incremental and marked by happenstance, much as was his road to power, but his focus on the Jewish menace was unrelenting, purposeful, and monomaniacal. During the 1930s, the pressure on the Jews in Germany became increasingly unbearable, as the extra-legal attacks that had begun on their businesses and public life became legal under the Nazis. The Nazi policy toward the Jews was, as the scholar Victor Klemperer wrote in his secret diary, "oppression, oppression, oppression."[22] The Nuremberg Laws, promulgated by the Nazis in July 1935, made it impossible for Jews to engage in most professions and to interact with German society in normal ways. Not only did these statutes define Jews according to hereditary ("racial") criteria, they also deprived Jews of German citizenship and thus of civil protection and legal recourse. As Klemperer put it, "one is an alien species or a Jew with 25 percent Jewish blood, if one grandparent was Jewish. As in 15th century Spain[,] but then the issue was faith. Today it's zoology and business." But, as Klemperer noted later in his diary, the Nazis' legal persecution of the Jews also provoked violence: "The Jew-baiting and pogrom atmosphere grow day by day."[23]

During *Reichskristallnacht*, the Night of the Broken Glass (November 9 and 10, 1938), the Nazis encouraged a widespread pogrom throughout Germany and parts of Austria against the Jews, as synagogues were set on fire, Jews were beaten in the streets, and Jewish shops were ransacked and pillaged. Some ninety-one Jews were killed and another thirty thousand were arrested before the disturbances, which began to get out of hand and engendered criticism from some Nazi officials (Hermann Göring at their head), were brought to an end by the authorities. The message was clear: the Jews were not welcome in Germany and should leave. Most of those who had the money and wherewithal to do so fled the country, many to neighboring France or to England, some to the United States or Palestine.

When Hitler invaded Poland on September 1, 1939 (followed by the Soviet occupation of the eastern part of Poland beginning on September 17), the dynamics of the Jewish question changed radically for the worse. Within a matter of months, millions of Jews fell under direct Nazi power, and a large proportion of them were traditional Orthodox and Hasidic Jews—*Ostjuden* (eastern Jews), for whom the Nazis and many Germans had abiding contempt. Hitler's invasion of Poland was followed by declarations of war by France and England on Germany, which meant that public opinion in the democracies of Western Europe ceased to deter Nazi policies regarding the Jews, to the very modest extent that it did before the outbreak of hostilities. Hitler's new partner in the east, Josef Stalin, certainly would make no representations on behalf of the Jews.

Hitler's genocidal policies in Poland were directed both at the Poles and at the Jews. At the outset of the occupation, in Operation Tannenberg, the Nazis identified some 60,000 leading Polish politicians, clergymen, teachers, lawyers, writers, and other prominent members of the Polish elite for arrest and elimination. The idea was to decapitate the Polish nation and force the remainder of the population into a subservient role as denationalized helots in the service of the Third Reich. Some Polish children were taken as "Aryans" to the Reich to be raised as Germans.

Soviet policy in occupied Poland had strong similarities to the Nazis in this connection. In three waves of arrests and deportations during 1940 and 1941, the Soviets sought to rid Poland of what they considered the "bourgeois" elite, government classes, and the "Polish Pans" (the nobles and landowners). Some 380,000 Poles—men, women, and children—were deported to remote locations in Siberia and Central Asia, while mostly Ukrainian, Belarusian, and local Jewish communists took their places in leading government, educational, and civic institutions. The Soviet decapitation of the Poles involved executing—with a shot into the back of the head—some 22,000 captured Polish officers, reserve officers, and government officials in April and May 1940, a horrendous crime known as the Katyn forest massacre.

The Nazi invasion of Poland forged a trail of suffering and death among Jews that would end in Auschwitz, Treblinka, and the killing fields of the east.[24] Polish Jews were deprived of their property and livelihood, and forced into overcrowded ghettos throughout the Nazi-administered *Generalgouvernement* of Poland. The rounded-up Jews received a minimum amount of food, with a caloric intake per capita that meant the gradual withering away of their bodies, hunger, and death. In these conditions, sickness broke out in the ghettos across the region. People died in ever growing numbers from what one victim, Dawid Sierakowiak, called in his Łódź diary "ghetto disease." He writes: "A person becomes thin (an 'hourglass') and pale in the face, then comes the swelling, a few days in bed or in the hospital, and that's it. The person was living, the person is dead; we live and die like cattle."[25]

On May 23, 1941, the *Information Bulletin* of the Polish underground published a description of the conditions in the Warsaw ghetto:

> Further crowding has resulted in conditions of ill-health, hunger and monstrous poverty that defy description. Groups of pale and emaciated people wander aimlessly through the overcrowded streets. Beggars sit and lie along the walls and the sight of people collapsing from starvation is common. The refuge for abandoned children takes in a dozen infants every day; every day a few more people die on the street. Contagious diseases are spreading, particularly tuberculosis. Meanwhile the Germans continue to plunder the wealthy Jews. Their treatment of the Jews is always exceptionally inhuman. They torment them and subject them constantly to their wild and bestial amusements.[26]

When the propaganda minister of the Third Reich, Josef Goebbels, saw films of the Warsaw Ghetto, he felt repulsed, he said, by the filthy and diseased condition of the subhuman Jews who lived there. "The Jews [*diese Judentum*] must be eliminated," he stated. Visiting the Łódź ghetto in October 1939, Goebbels wrote: "These are no longer people, they are animals. This is therefore not a humanitarian but a surgical task. One must make incisions, extremely radical ones."[27] In short, the Nazis created the very conditions among the Jews in the ghettos that confirmed their own genocidal inclinations.

On June 22, 1941, the Nazi armies attacked the Soviet Union in Operation Barbarossa, and in a spectacular series of encircling operations, inflicted severe, if not fatal, setbacks on the Red Army. Hitler and his generals thought that the war was as good as over. Many in the West did, as well. Millions of Red Army soldiers were taken prisoner and placed in camps, which turned into genocidal hellholes for captured officers and soldiers. Jewish officers were shot on the spot. Some 3.3 million Soviet POWs died in German camps (out of 5.7 million captured). On the eve of the attack, Hitler had issued his infamous Commissars' Order to the SS Einsatzgruppen that gave the elite Nazi paramilitary formations license to eliminate the political leadership of the Red Army, which he equated with the Jews. By slating "Jewish-Bolsheviks" for execution, Hitler was, in effect, giving the SS units license to murder Jews, which they did in the wake of the Wehrmacht's advance.

In the early months following the invasion, the Nazis encouraged local populations—Lithuanians, Poles, Ukrainians, Belarusians, and others—to engage in pogroms against their Jewish neighbors. Traditional anti-Semitic sentiments among segments of these populations were inflamed by the Nazis' propaganda messages about Jewish inferiority and perfidy. In the territories of eastern Poland and the Baltic region previously occupied by the Soviet Union, some local Jews had welcomed the Soviet invasion and took part willingly in the new communist-run administrations. The perception among the local population that Jews strongly sympathized with the Soviets was much more powerful than the reality of Jewish collaboration. Before evacuating eastern Poland, the People's Commissariat for Internal Affairs (NKVD) shot many of the political prisoners held in their jails. Finding the sometimes tortured and disfigured corpses of the victims, the local populations blamed the outrages on the Jews, and sought revenge. In Kaunas (Kovno), Lviv, Vilnius (Wilno), and many smaller towns stretching across the territory first occupied by the Soviets and then the Germans, fierce pogroms took the lives thousands of Jews.

The numbers killed in the pogroms do not do justice to the horrors of persecution, humiliation, beatings, rape, and torture that the Jews were forced to endure at the hands of their countrymen of various nationalities. Sometimes, the perpetrators were members of nationalist militias that had quickly formed to advance the interests of the local populations under Nazi rule.[28] Sometimes, as in the incineration of the

Jewish population of Jedwabne in northeastern Poland, the perpetrators were simply townspeople, men, women, and even children.[29] The atrocities committed against the Jews were unimaginably brutal. They set a pattern of behavior of local populations toward the Jews during the Nazi occupation that often made it seem to the Jewish victims that their persecutors were less the Germans than they were the Poles, Ukrainians, Belarusians, Lithuanians, Latvians, or others.

As the summer of 1941 progressed, the execution of the Jews by special SS units, the Einsatzgruppen, became increasingly frequent in the German-occupied territories. Though the pace and extent of the killing varied from place to place, depending on the fanaticism and diligence of the local army and SS commanders, by the beginning of the fall of 1941 the genocide became more all-encompassing, including women, children, and the elderly. As in Poland, the Jews of Ukraine, Belarus, and Lithuania had been confined to ghettos and marked for maltreatment and gradual starvation. At the same time, the Wehrmacht, the SS, and their local helpmates marched Jews to execution sites, forced them sometimes to dig their own mass graves, and shot them in the hundreds of thousands throughout the region. In December 1941, Colonel Jäger reported the killing actions by his SS group:

> Today I can confirm that Strike Commando 3 has reached the goal of solving the Jewish problem in Lithuania. The only remaining Jews are laborers and their families. The implementation of such actions is in the first instance an organizational problem. The Jews had to be collected in one or more towns and a ditch had to be dug at the right site for the right number.... The Jews were brought in groups of 500, separated by at least 1.2 miles, to the place of execution.... Only careful planning enable the Commando to carry out up to 5 actions a week and at the same time continue the work in Kovno [Kaunas] without interruption.[30]

As for the remaining Jews necessary for the work force, Col. Jäger noted: "I am of the opinion that the male work Jews should be sterilized immediately to prevent any procreation. A Jewess who nevertheless becomes pregnant is to be liquidated."[31]

There was no single order from Hitler indicating that all the Jews should be killed. But the signals of Hitler's wishes, and those of the Nazi leadership, became clear by mid-fall 1941. The shortage of food in the occupied areas became increasingly noticeable from the late summer on, contributing to the sense among Nazi officials that the Jews and other "useless eaters" should be eliminated.[32] There was also the process of "working toward the Führer," meaning the Nazi leaders in the field felt

After the German invasion of the Soviet Union in June 1941, mobile execution squads, police, and military units, sometimes aided by local collaborators, shot large numbers of Soviet citizens, as shown in this photograph. The victims were executed over ditches, ravines, or trenches, sometimes dug by the victims themselves, and buried in mass graves. The Germans murdered more than a million Soviet Jews in this way, including 34,000 at Babi Yar, on the outskirts of Kyiv, on September 29–30, 1941. History/The Image Works

they were doing Hitler's bidding—and fulfilling his many prophecies about the destruction of the Jews if there were a war—by executing Jews.[33] The mass murderers certainly received no orders countermanding their actions. On the contrary, those SS and Wehrmacht officials who were in charge of killing the Jews received affirmation and promotion for their deeds.

The Nazi advance on Moscow stalled in November and December 1941, indicating that the war would be much more protracted than Hitler had initially anticipated. The Red Army was proving a tenacious foe. Given that the Germans occupied great swaths of Ukrainian and Belarusian territory containing the majority of the Soviet Jewish population, the Nazi killing machine continued its pursuit of the elimination of the Jews throughout 1942 and 1943, when the Red Army began to push the Wehrmacht out of Soviet territory. In January 1942, the infamous Wannsee Conference took place on the outskirts of Berlin to determine the fate of Europe's Jews. With representatives from the various bureaucracies, including the notorious Reinhard Heydrich and Adolf Eichmann from the SS, to coordinate the "final solution," a plan was drawn up to transport Jews throughout Europe to the death camps in occupied Poland at Chełmno, Bełżec, Sobibor, Auschwitz-Birkenau, Majdanek, and Treblinka, where gas chambers were to be used to kill Jews and ovens to destroy their corpses. The horrors of the death camps and the attack on the human personality that they represented have been frequently described in Holocaust literature. Few images touch the soul of the reader more than Primo Levi's description of the "Musselman," a term used in the camps to describe his fellow prisoners in Auschwitz on the verge of dying:

> All the musselmans who finished in the gas chambers have the same story, or more exactly, have no story; they followed the slope down to the bottom, like streams that run down to the sea. On their entry into the camp, through basic incapacity or by misfortune, or through some banal incident, they are overcome before they can adapt themselves.... Their life is short, but their number is endless: they, the Musselmänner, the drowned, form the backbone of the camp, an anonymous mass, continually renewed and always identical, of non-men who march and labour in silence, the divine spark dead within them, already too empty to really suffer. One hesitates to call them living: one hesitates to call their death death, in the face of which they have no fear, for they are too tired to understand.
>
> They crowd my memory with their faceless presences, and if I could enclose all the evil of our time in one image, I would choose this image which is familiar to me: an emaciated man, with head dropped and shoulders curved, on whose face and in whose eyes not a trace of a thought is to be seen.[34]

The gruesome "industrial" phase of the Holocaust killed some 2 million Jews in the gas chambers; the exact number is still disputed.[35] Another 3.5 million Jews were shot, starved, or died of disease. Even when it became obvious that the Germans had lost the war, the murder of the Jews went on. There was no let up, as the Nazis deported Hungarian and Greek Jews to Auschwitz, and chased down Jews in remote islands in the Mediterranean and in mountain where they tried to hide. As the Soviet armies drove westward, the German authorities murdered Jews who could not be moved and forced others into death marches, which took countless additional lives.

Hitler's genocide against the Jews took place in the context of his attacks on mentally and physically disabled Germans, homosexuals, and Sinti and Roma. Along with the Jews, whom the Nazis considered the archenemies of the German nation, these other groups were accused of threatening the health and integrity of German society. The disabled were the first to be targeted in the so-called T-4 or euthanasia program; indeed, they were killed in very large numbers—as many as 200,000—mostly before the invasion of the Soviet Union. The first use of gas, usually from bottles of carbon monoxide, against victims of the Nazi regime was recorded in 1939, when the disabled were eliminated in gas chambers and gas wagons. The Nazi elimination of the people with mental and physical disabilities would have been completed in Nazi Germany if the parents and families of the victims had not made uncomfortable protests to the government about the deaths of their relatives at the hands of the medical establishment.

The Sinti and Roma suffered a fate much more akin to that of the Jews and, like the attempted elimination of the disabled, it should be called genocide. Deemed racially inferior by the Nazi authorities, the Sinti and Roma were deported from Germany to camps in the east. Although not immediately slated for elimination with the invasion of the Soviet Union, as were all the Jews, they were subjected to widespread medical experiments, starved to death, and sometimes shot on the spot. A special camp for the Sinti and Roma was set up at Auschwitz, where many thousands were sent to the gas chambers. Of the 20,000 or so Sinti and Roma who lived in Germany before the war, only 5,000 survived. Throughout Europe, the Nazis killed some 200,000 Sinti and Roma, in the process inflicting fearsome cruelties on many who managed to survive.

The numbers of people killed in the genocides of the first half of the twentieth century grew exponentially, while the brutality involved appears to be depressingly consistent. The number of victims swelled as the technology of mass murder became increasingly efficient and sophisticated. The German Army in South West Africa executed Herero and Nama, but the majority of their deaths came from starvation and disease, as it did in the cases of the settler genocides that were considered in the previous chapter. General von Trotha intentionally drove his enemies into the desert, so that they would die from thirst, hunger, and exposure, much as did the Young Turk government to the Armenians and Syriac Christians. Certainly, the Nazis assumed a unique place among the long list of genocidaires by purposely devising methods of industrial killing—the use of gas wagons, gas chambers, and crematoria to dispose of the bodies—that were unprecedented in the history of genocide and have not been employed since. They were able to kill so many people in part because they employed a well-equipped paramilitary force deployed by the SS, which was specifically charged with accomplishing the murderous task. They also used an elaborate rail system to transport victims to the death camps, which themselves were organized to kill as many people as possible as quickly as possible. But one should also not forget that the majority of the Jews were executed in groups and buried in mass graves, a method that characterized genocide from its very beginning.

CHAPTER 6

Communist Genocides

The 1948 U.N. Convention on the Prevention and Punishment of Genocide, the foundational legal document defining genocide, limited the categories of its victims to national, ethnic, religious, or racial groups. Attempts to include social and political groups in the convention were defeated in good part because of the opposition of the Soviet delegation to the United Nations, which worried that its repression of social and political groups at home might be considered genocidal.[1] Since that time, it has been difficult to think about genocide as a crime against a social or political group or, for that matter, of other identifiable groups of co-nationals like, for example, homosexuals or handicapped people in the case of the Nazis.

How, then, does one deal with the Cambodian genocide (1975–1979), when nearly 1.7 million Cambodians (a total of 21 percent of the country's population) were driven into the countryside, interned in frightful prison camps, and died in huge numbers from starvation, disease, and exposure brought on by the policies of the Khmer Rouge regime?[2] Where do the millions of Chinese deaths during the Great Leap Forward—estimates of the death toll range between 30 million and 47 million—fit into a history of mass killing and genocide?[3] How does one think in comparative terms about the campaigns of Stalin against "kulaks" (allegedly rich farmers), political opponents, Ukrainian peasants, and "socially harmful" people? The answer suggested here is to apply the category of "communist genocide" to understand these events.

Beginning in May 1922, Vladimir Ilyich Lenin, the leader of the Bolshevik Revolution and ruler of Russia, suffered a series of strokes that left him incapacitated, and he finally died in January 1924. Josef Stalin, a gifted political infighter and convincing party comrade, managed to outmaneuver the other members of the Politburo, including the brilliant if politically inept Lev Trotsky, and seized control of the destiny of the Bolshevik Party. Stalin won the struggle for power with a brutal forcefulness and determination that would characterize his rule from the late 1920s until his death in March 1953. He also demonstrated a capacity to make allies when he needed them and to abandon them without the least hesitation when they became expendable. Especially during the crucial period of forced-pace industrialization and collectivization from the end of 1928 to 1933, Stalin employed his political acuity and ruthlessness to isolate his opponents in the Politburo and then to cut away methodically at their prestige and influence.[4]

Stalin's violence against the Soviet people took the form of fierce retribution for their lack of understanding of, and opposition to, the wisdom of his policies. The failures of collectivization were blamed on the kulaks, a group of purportedly rich peasants who supposedly exploited the poor and sabotaged the collectivization campaign. Kulaks were identified as the class enemy, and discontented peasants, rich or poor, rural clergy, and other village denizens who opposed collectivization were included in this category. On March 15, 1931, the OGPU (security police) issued a memorandum on the kulaks, which stated that the goal of the campaign was "to totally cleanse" the agricultural regions. The most dangerous kulaks would be "immediately eliminated," the others sent into exile. "We will exile the kulak by the thousands and when necessary—shoot the kulak breed," pronounced one of the slogans in the countryside. "We will make soap out of the kulaks," stated another. A third declared: "Our class enemy must be wiped off the face of the earth."[5] Gangs of party members, rural poor, and local thugs attacked and brutalized alleged kulaks. An OGPU reported noted: "These people drove the dekulakized naked in the streets, beat them, organized drinking-bouts in their houses, shot over their heads, forced them to dig their own graves, undressed women and searched them, stole valuables, money, etc."[6] Some 30,000 kulaks were shot, while as many as 10 million were forced from their homes, perhaps 2 million of those sent into exile.

For Soviet officials, the social category of kulaks took on hereditary and even racial characteristics. Kulaks were deported (and died) as families, and surviving children, and even grandchildren, of kulaks carried that mark of Cain for the rest of their lives. This was, wrote Aleksandr Solzhenitsyn, the essence of Stalin's plan: "the peasant's seed must perish together with the adults."[7] In official denunciations, kulaks were labeled "enemies of the people." But they were also dehumanized as "swine," "dogs," and "cockroaches"; they were scum, vermin, and filth, to be cleansed, crushed, and eliminated. The writer Maxim Gorky called them "half-animals," while the Soviet press frequently depicted them as apes.[8]

When Stalin said he wanted to wipe out the kulaks as a class, he meant it literally. The special settlements to which they were exiled were poorly provisioned, if at all; materials for housing were scarce; medical assistance was lacking; the cold penetrated everywhere; escape often meant death. One frustrated official of the camp administration talked about his ill-fated attempts in January 1932 to secure provisions for his camp from the district party chief:

> Furious, he told me: "Comrade Shpek, you don't understand anything about the policies of our government! Do you really think that these elements have been sent here to be reeducated? No, Comrade, we have to see to it that by spring they're all dead, even if we have to be clever about it: dress them in such a way that they'll at least cut down a little wood before they die. You can see for yourself in what condition they send them to us here, disembarking them on the riverbank in rags, naked—if the government really wanted to reeducate them, it would clothe them without our help!" ... After this conversation, I refused to organize the camp, for I had understood that they were going to send people out there and that I was supposed to see to it that they all died.[9]

Many tens of thousands of kulaks died from hunger, exposure, and disease in exile. In January 1932, the OGPU estimated that close to a half million kulaks, roughly 30 percent of the kulak deportees at that time, had either died or run away.[10]

A second wave of "repression" of the kulaks came in July 1937, in conjunction with Order 00447, which was also intended to remove from society "asocial" elements (alleged prostitutes, chronically unemployed, alcoholics, gamblers, street people, et al.) and "former people"—anyone associated with the previous regime: nobles, former government servants, and members of non-Bolshevik political parties. Those kulaks who had managed to flee persecution in the countryside and had found work in the cities were arrested, some executed, and the rest sent to the Gulag, the Main Administration of Corrective Labor Camps and Labor Settlements, where many perished of hunger, disease, and exposure.

The countryside deteriorated badly as a consequence of the de-kulakization campaign and forced collectivization. Yet the government's demands for grain procurement did not slacken. The basic idea was to sell the grain abroad to raise the capital necessary for the expansion of industry, according to the First Five-Year Plan. As severe shortages of grain appeared in the countryside and the peasants kept their grain for their own consumption, the authorities responded with draconian measures, including confiscating seed grain and taking the collective farms' reserves. This in turn sparked a fierce famine all over the Soviet Union that caused widespread misery and death.

The famine in Ukraine was particularly severe. Part of the problem was that the Ukrainian peasants were stalwart opponents of collectivization, successfully resisting requisition in every way possible. This aroused Stalin's ire and led to especially harsh policies carried out against entire subregions and designated villages of Ukraine. Added to the dangerous genocidal mixture was Stalin's animus toward Ukrainian national consciousness, which the Soviet leadership attributed to the backwardness of the Ukrainian peasantry. In the 1920s, Soviet policies of "indigenization" (*korenizatsiia*) had encouraged the Ukrainians to pursue their culture, language, and distinctive historical background as a way to promote the integration of revolutionary Ukraine into the new Union of Soviet Socialist Republics. But Stalin and his lieutenants came to the realization by the beginning of the 1930s that this policy had created serious obstacles to the Kremlin's control of the republic and to their ability to dictate social and economic policies as they saw fit. While the Soviet leaders did not completely drop indigenization, they now made efforts to gut the policy of serious political consequences.

The grain crisis in the Ukrainian countryside overlapped with Stalin's intent to deprive Ukrainians of their ability to function as an independent entity. Stalin insisted that the Ukrainian party not back off of collection norms: "No manner of deviation—regarding either amounts or deadlines set for grain deliveries—can be permitted from the plan established for your region." As the hunger in the villages intensified, Stalin ordered that a "knockout blow" be delivered to those collective farms that continued to resist requisitioning. Those who did not work—the so-called idlers—could starve, as far as he was concerned.[11] Peasants who attempted to leave their hungry villages were forced to return, borders with other republics were sealed, and roadblocks were set up to prevent peasants from seeking food in the towns and cities. The Kremlin ignored the death agony of the Ukrainian countryside, as millions of peasants suffered from hunger and disease. Stalin told the writer Mikhail Sholokhov, who attempted to appeal to Stalin about the hunger: "The fact that this sabotage was silent and appeared to be quite peaceful (there was no bloodshed) changes nothing—these people deliberately tried to undermine the Soviet state. It is a fight to the death, Comrade Sholokhov."[12]

The horrible fate of death by starvation was the central human fact of the Holodomor (the "killer famine," as Ukrainians call it.) The reports of people going mad with hunger and engaging in cannibalism and necrophagy reached Stalin and his Kremlin helpmates, as they did the Ukrainian party leaders. Excerpts from a July 1933 report by the Italian consul in Kharkiv capture some of the misery of the countryside:

> The current situation in Ukraine is horrific ... the countryside is engulfed in famine, typhus and dysentery. There are also cases of cholera and even plague.... As for sanitary conditions, they can be no worse than their current state. Doctors are prohibited from speaking about typhus and death from starvation. People who are unable to secure bread (very black bread with various additives) gradually grow weaker and die of heart failure without any signs of disease.... There are frequent cases of hallucinations when people mistake children for animals, slaughter and eat them. Those who managed to regain their strength using this kind of food did not recall wanting to eat their own children, and denied ever having such intentions.[13]

The Ukrainians lost all hope; the famine was not even recognized as such; the government turned down all offers of relief from abroad as unnecessary.

The horrors that ensued in the Ukrainian countryside, the Holodomor, should be considered genocide. Stalin was out to demolish the Ukrainian peasants, whom he saw as the backbone of Ukrainian consciousness. He could not starve them all to death; there was simply too much Ukrainian land that needed farmhands to plant and sow. But he could break the back of Ukrainian resistance by reducing the peasantry to a whimpering mass of starving and dying humanity. This he did without the least sense of regret or second thoughts.

Stalin's attack on the Ukrainian peasantry shared some of the characteristics of Stalin's genocidal policies toward the Poles and Germans, among other nationalities in the Soviet Union, during the 1930s and early 1940s. Stalin's paranoid visions of Polish legions pouring across the Soviet border in the early 1930s led him to arrest and execute large numbers of Poles who lived in the border regions and to remove the rest to Siberia. His campaign against the Poles continued throughout the 1930s. During the Great Purges of 1937–38, Stalin again targeted the Poles for special repressions. It was reported that the Leningrad NKVD scoured the local phone book to identify and arrest those citizens with Polish names. In the end, some 144,000 people were arrested in the Polish operation; 110,000 were shot, even including many Polish communists.[14]

Soviet German communities had been in Russian and Ukrainian territory since Catherine the Great had invited them to settle in the empire at the end of the eighteenth century. By the beginning of the

1930s, they, like the Poles, were deemed enemies of the Soviet people and subjected to forced deportation and execution. In the German operation in 1937–38, as many as 68,000 people were arrested; 43,000 of them were condemned to death. Later, the peoples of the northern Caucasus were accused of collaboration with the Germans during the war, and were deported from their homelands to Kazakhstan and Uzbekistan. In the case of the Chechens-Ingush, the conditions of deportation and exile took on genocidal proportions, as the malicious indifference of the authorities to the welfare of the "punished peoples" ended up killing hundreds of thousands of Chechens and Ingush. Starvation, disease, and exposure also took the lives of some 75,000 Crimean Tatars out of the 189,000 who were deported—and who, like the Chechens and Ingush, were taken in an overnight operation from their homeland in the Crimea to the inhospitable and alien reaches of Central Asia.[15]

The "Great Terror" of 1937–38 is hard to classify as genocide because ethnic, national, racial, religious, or even self-identified social and political groups were not attacked as such. Instead, Stalin moved against alleged political opponents (including their friends, relatives, and supposed adherents) who were designated by the regime as clandestine bands of political enemies, and thus eliminated on that basis. Soviet citizens were enjoined to suspect their neighbors, friends, and even relatives, and denounce them as "enemies of the people." Men and women were picked up off the streets or taken from their apartments in the middle of the night to be interrogated, tortured, and forced to sign fake confessions. Certain categories of alleged class enemies were doomed to arrest, summary trial, and death or exile to the Gulag. Stalin set the tone for the terror. In a response to a toast to "the Great Stalin" at Kliment Voroshilov's apartment (November 7, 1937), he proposed his own toast:

> Whosoever attempts to destroy that unity of the socialist state, whoever seeks the separation of any of its part of nationalities—that man is an enemy, a sworn enemy of the state and peoples of the USSR. And we will destroy each and every such enemy, even if he was an old Bolshevik; we will destroy all his kin, his family. We will mercilessly destroy anyone who, by his deeds or thoughts—yes, his thoughts—threatens the unity of the socialist state. To the complete destruction of all enemies, themselves, and their kind! (Approving exclamations: To the Great Stalin!)[16]

According to one recent estimate, some 800,000 people were executed in the Great Purge over a period of sixteen months: 50,000 executions per month, or 1,700 per day for almost 500 days.[17] Hundreds of thousands more disappeared into the system of prisons, special settlements, and forced labor camps of the Gulag system.

Stalin died in March 1953, and his successor, Nikita Khrushchev, introduced a wave of de-Stalinization in his "Secret Speech" of February 25, 1956, which condemned the dictator's crimes and his "cult of personality." In China, Mao Zedong's initial reaction to these events was to allow expression of criticism under the "Hundred Flowers" campaign, which he launched in May 1956. This was his way to control the bureaucratization of the state apparatus, keep the party alert to social needs, and gain the support of intellectuals and scientists for his modernization programs. But the uprisings in Eastern Europe in 1956, provoked in part by Khrushchev's speech, and the sharpness of internal Chinese criticisms, strike movements, and student protests, convinced him that he had to change course in mid-1957, when he launched an "anti-rightist" campaign that effectively closed down all overt opposition to the regime. Meanwhile, Khrushchev's statements about moving the Soviet Union into the final stage of communism and surpassing the United States in steel production seemed to inspire Mao to even more radical goals. He claimed in November 1957 that China would surpass British steel production in ten years. But Mao also looked with a jaundiced eye at Khrushchev's claims that communism would be achieved in the Soviet Union.

Instead of accepting Soviet leadership, Mao launched a campaign in the spring of 1958 for the full collectivization of agriculture, eliminating private plots, forcing Chinese peasants into huge communes, and seizing their personal property in the name of communal egalitarianism. Stated one enthusiastic party chief: "the dream of Utopia of our predecessors will come to fruition and be surpassed."[18] Part of Mao's program included the building of numerous small backyard steel foundries in the communes, which would make possible, the party claimed, the doubling of steel production within a year. The party set up communal kitchens as a way to control peasants' food consumption and eliminate the importance of the family as a production unit. Local party officials seized the peasants' kitchen utensils and pots and pans to be melted down in the backyard steel foundries. Already by October, the party had forced more than 90 percent of the peasants into some 26,000 communes, with an average of 5,000 households. Within a year, 99 percent of the peasants were transferred into communes.

If these huge changes were not disruptive enough to the rural economy, Mao also introduced a series of mammoth water, dam, and other infrastructure projects that required hundreds of millions of workers from the countryside, taking them away from farming while, at the same time, destroying millions of acres of agricultural land. The Chinese also adopted some of the worst practices of Soviet agriculture made popular by the pseudo-scientific agronomist Trofim Lysenko. Especially his ideas of close and deep planting, instead of China's traditional extensive agriculture, wasted seed and left fallow otherwise fertile land.

The famine that resulted from the combination of these policies of the Great Leap Forward first became obvious in the early fall of 1958, when the harvest fell far short of what was necessary to provide minimal sustenance for peasants in many parts of the country. By all accounts, the weather was normal in the years of the famine, though there were reports of the destruction of crops by locusts. When faced with calls from the party to lower the requisition levels in late 1958 and early 1959, Mao responded—much as Stalin had done during the famine of 1932–33—that the peasants were simply concealing grain and that procurement levels should be increased. Mao's indifference to the fierce suffering of the peasantry—tens of millions of deaths, widespread cannibalism, mass suicide, and disease, among other woes—was amply documented by his presentation at the Shanghai conference, March 25, 1959. When party leader Li Xiannian suggested that it would be a good idea to give more priority in agriculture to the domestic over the foreign market, Mao responded: "There are times when domestic trading should be subjected to export needs.... We should eat and consume less. We should live frugally to guarantee the export market." Mao's idea was to pay off the country's debt to the Soviet Union as soon as possible.[19]

At the Shanghai meeting Mao also tacitly promised that the Chinese elites, the party cadres in particular, would not suffer from any shortage of food, while the peasants would die, perhaps even should die, in large numbers. He said: "To distribute resources evenly will only ruin the Great Leap Forward. Where there is not enough to eat, people starve to death. It is better to let half the people die so that the other half can eat their fill."[20]

For more than three years, reports came into the capital from all over the countryside of the terrible suffering of the Chinese peasantry. Entire regions were consumed by the famine, many with death rates far exceeding 50 percent. Hunger haunted the land, as some peasants turned to cannibalism to survive. The documented reports of cannibalism were terse. But each contained a terrible story of desperate hunger:

> Date: February 25, 1960. Location: Yaohejia village in Hongtai commune.
>
> Culprit's name: Yan Zhongsheng. Culprit's status: Poor peasant. Victim's name: Yang Sansun. Relation to the culprit: Younger brother.
>
> Number of victims: 1. Manner of crime: Killed the victim and consumed the body.
>
> Reason: To survive.[21]

A local medical inspector, Liang Zhiyuan, who thoroughly documented mortality in the villages of Bo County, reported frequent cases of cannibalism: "The extensiveness of the practice, the number of incidents, and the length of time that it continued is exceptional in human history.... There was not a single commune where cannibalism was not discovered, and in some production brigades not a single village was untouched by the phenomenon."[22]

Every imaginable source of sustenance—bark, tree roots, leaves, grass, rats, wall paint, and even the earth itself—was consumed by starving peasants. "In some localities," wrote one medical expert, "the bones of animals that had died years ago were gathered up, smashed into fragments, and boiled into soup," in the desperate (if vain) hope of getting some nutrition.[23] Sometimes the peasants were killed by what they ate. Untold thousands died of eating poisonous plants and mushrooms. Sometimes they died of diseases brought on by the hunger: typhus, dysentery, diarrhea, and others.

Families sold everything they had in order to get some food. Sometimes they even sold their children. Daughters, especially, were sold to families as child brides. Many girls migrated to the cities, engaging in prostitution in order to eat.[24] In the countryside itself, rape and other forms of sexual abuse accompanied the hunger. Women and girls were defenseless against the arbitrary power of the cadres, and were sometimes forced to strip naked and parade in front of the bosses.[25]

Reminiscent of Ukraine in the 1932–33, so-called dissuasion stations were set up along roadways, at train and bus stations, and at river crossings to stop hungry peasants from fleeing their villages. When some party leaders tried to protest the policies that had created the misery and death in the first place, Mao responded by intensifying the anti-rightist campaign, which effectively strangled all criticism. Even though he knew of the problems of the hunger in detail, Mao would frequently wax eloquent about the accomplishments of the Great Leap Forward. In a poem about his hometown village of Shaoshan, Mao tied the romantic accomplishments of the present with the Hunan peasant uprisings of 1927:

> Cursed by the flow of memories,
> I am back in my native place thirty-two years ago.
> Red flags flutter from the spears of the enslaved peasants,
> As the landlords raise their whips in cruel hands.
> It took many sacrifices to make us strong
> That we dared tell sun and moon to bring a new day.
> In delight I watch the waving rows of rice and beans,
> While all around the heroes return through the evening haze.[26]

He also initiated an "anti-hiding" campaign against those same "heroes" to seize the grain and produce they supposedly concealed from the party. As late as November 1960, Mao still insisted that the problems in the countryside were caused by hidden enemies who needed to be flushed out in renewed "class struggle."[27]

That Mao blamed the peasants for their own misery emboldened local cadres to beat the peasants physically into complete submission, as if their torment would somehow lessen the suffering. "In some communes," noted one report, "'beating frenzy' is like an evil wind sweeping through society from the top down."[28] The most common instruments for the beatings were heavy sticks that, in some cases, killed the victims. One commune reported that more than 70 percent of the peasants had been battered during the "Anti-Hiding Campaign":

> Any commune Party secretary, or brigade leader, or even administrator can beat people up, deprive them of food, and loot their homes. Many villagers have been beaten or starved to death. No one is spared, from elderly people to young workers and even five- or six-year-old children. Cadres not only physically assaulted people themselves but encouraged villagers to beat up villagers, and children to beat up children. In some areas, there are even special "people-beating squads."[29]

In Daoxian county, in Hunan, 10 percent of the many thousands of deaths were attributed by an investigative team to peasants having been beaten to death, buried alive, or killed in other ways by militia and party members. In the Fengle commune, 17 percent died in a single year; 65 percent of the deaths were caused by being beaten, starved, or forced to commit suicide by the local cadres.[30]

Routine beatings were sometimes also accompanied by torture. A 1961 report from Sichuan province noted: "The methods of torture included hanging people up, beating them, forcing them to kneel on burning charcoal, piercing their mouths, clipping off their fingers, stitching their lips, pushing needles into the nipples, force-feeding them feces, stuffing dried beans down their throats and so on." The party cadres, added the same report, "tried every possible means to break down the peasants emotionally as well as physically." They sometimes deprived the peasants of the meager sustenance that was available to them, starving them to death in the process, just to demonstrate the cadres' power over the villages. Local party officials sometimes had the same attitude toward life and death as did Mao: "A few deaths are nothing. . . . There are too many people in our country, the more people who die, the more food for us to eat."[31]

Although the cities were not immune to food shortages and famine, and the inevitable corruption and degradation that accompanied them, the Chinese countryside had sunk into a swamp of brutality, hunger, rape, desperation, and death. When the president of China, Liu Shaoqi, traveled to his home village in Hunan province in April 1961, he was shocked by the conditions he found there and the terrible damage inflicted by the government policies on the local communes. When returning to Beijing, he took up the cause of trying to alleviate the misery of the countryside, though he focused on the problems of implementation of the Great Leap Forward, *not* on the party line itself. Still, in his speech to the gathering of the Central Committee leadership on May 31, 1961, and in his three-hour presentation to the "Seven Thousand Cadres Conference" in January 1962, Liu Shaoqi made it clear that party errors had created the problems in the countryside. The famine was not simply the result of natural factors or of peasant malfeasance, as had earlier been claimed:

> The problem in the past few years was caused by unrealistic grain-collecting quotas, unrealistic estimates, unrealistic procurement figures, and unrealistic workloads. . . . Was the disaster [in the past few years] a natural calamity? In Hunan people say that three-tenths was natural calamity and seven-tenths was man-made. . . . Throughout the country quite a few errors have been made while implementing [party policies]. Although in some places the disaster is indeed a natural calamity, I don't think we can use only one finger to describe our setbacks.[32]

Liu's audience was apparently shocked by the temerity of even mentioning the term "man-made disaster" to describe the catastrophe that had engulfed the countryside.[33]

Despite Mao's foot-dragging and indifference to the suffering and death stalking the Chinese countryside, Liu Shaoqi's efforts made it possible for other party bosses to propose ways of ameliorating the pressure from the center on food requisitions and in allowing some market conditions to help create incentives for peasants to produce. Private property was returned to the peasants, and the backyard steel foundries were abandoned. By the end of 1962, the famine finally came to an end. Birth rates started to rise again, and death rates started to fall from the appalling heights of a few years earlier. "The population growth rate," states one document from Sichuan province, "has become more or less normal."[34] Mao had to back off from his policies, since his popularity and position in the party were unquestionably diminished. But it is clear in retrospect that Mao was biding his time. There was one confrontation between Mao and Liu that indicated Mao's deep displeasure. Liu insisted to Mao in a private talk in July 1962 that two critics of the Great Leap Forward be allowed to present their ideas about land distribution. Mao was outraged. But Liu insisted: "So many people have died of hunger! ... History will judge you and me, even cannibalism will go into the books."[35]

Just as the experience of the Soviet Union was central to the development of the Chinese Revolution and its Great Leap Forward, the ideas and programs of the Communist Party of Kampuchea (the CPK) and its leader Saloth Sar (Pol Pot) owed a great deal to the model and active support of the Chinese. The Khmer Rouge saw its task as building socialism in a "fast 'Leap Forward.' "[36] It seems, too, that the apocalyptic millenarianism that characterized Mao's thinking as he entered the period of the Great Leap Forward had a deep effect on the Cambodian communists, whose overwhelming commitment to founding a new world completely disconnected from the supposed degenerate realities of the past surpassed even the Chinese. All three "experiments" with establishing societies on totally new economic and class foundations— Stalinist, Maoist, and Pol Potist—failed miserably, while causing the deaths of millions of people in their own countries.

The U.S. carpet bombing in 1969 of the Cambodian sanctuaries used by the North Vietnamese to attack South Vietnam polarized the government of Prince Norodom Sihanouk, separating those who tried, like Sihanouk himself, to maintain distance from both the Americans and the North Vietnamese. General Lon Nol, a long-time member of the Sihanouk government, ousted the prince in a 1970 coup and established a decidedly pro-U.S. pseudo-democracy, known as the Khmer Republic. While Sihanouk fled the country for China, Lon Nol engaged in an extensive and brutal civil war against the communist Khmer Rouge forces. The more the United States bombed Cambodian villages and intervened on the ground, the more the Khmer Rouge seemed to garner support from Cambodian peasants. With the cooperation and help of the Vietnamese communists, Pol Pot and the Khmer Rouge defeated Lon Nol in 1975 and seized Phnom Penh. Lon Nol himself barely escaped the clutches of the Khmer Rouge, who had threatened to execute him and his entire government, and he made his way to the United States. Most members of his government and their families were not so lucky, and died at the hands of the Khmer Rouge.

The extreme radicalism of the Khmer Rouge became immediately apparent. After cutting off Phnom Penh from supplies during the last year of the civil war and bombarding the city with artillery, the Khmer Rouge called for the complete evacuation of the city. The city's population, now some 2 million people, swelled by many hundreds of thousands of refugees who had fled to the capital during the civil war, were forced out of their homes and sent to the countryside for "purifying" work. Sometimes the evacuees were told they would be able to return; sometimes they were told the evacuation was because American B-52s would bomb the city; sometimes they were told flat out that they would be killed.[37] "The expulsion of the population of Phnom Penh," the Khmer Rouge bragged, "is a measure one does not find in the revolution of any other country. This is an extraordinary measure aimed at the total overthrow of the feudal system and the capitalist system. In dispersing the city population to the countryside, we deal a decisive blow to the old order, and we transform all the towns of the country into worker towns. This is better than ever."[38]

Phnom Penh, the once beautiful and graceful "Pearl of Asia," became the capital of the Khmer Rouge regime and a home to torture and death. According to one witness, the fall of Phnom Penh was marked by the execution of two thousand Lon Nol soldiers with blows from bamboo sticks "to save bullets," after which the victims were buried in mass graves.[39] Many of the older and weaker evacuees died in the forced marches to the countryside.

The Khmer Rouge arrested members of the Lon Nol government and of the army and police, either executing them right away or incarcerating them in the infamous S-21 prison camp at the former Tuol Sleng High School. The political elite of the previous government was executed there or at several designated "killing fields" outside of the city after having been brutally tortured at S-21. The prison camp was commanded by Comrade Duch, Kaing Guek Eav, who, according to the Extraordinary Court for Cambodia, was responsible for a host of crimes against humanity, including conducting medical experiments on prisoners, extracting their blood, systematically torturing them until they confessed to their crimes, raping female internees, and supervising mass executions. One former prison official described the executions:

> After being interrogated, all the prisoners, whether they confessed or not, were killed on the spot, either just outside the prison, or in a paddy field in Prey So village.... To kill the victims, they ordered pits to be dug ahead of time ... each pit being 4 meters long, 2 meters wide, and 1.5 meters deep. They ordered us to take the prisoners one by one to up near the pits, where they were hit on the neck or on the head with iron bars that were nearly one meter long. After that, Pol Pot men cut the victims' throats or ripped their bellies open to pluck out the liver. Then the bodies were thrown into the pits and covered over. At first, 5 or 6 people were killed each day, but the number shot up day by day, and by 1977 the Pol-Pot–Ieng Sary gang had killed from 130 to 150 prisoners a day.[40]

The Khmer Rouge and its "Angkor" government, which referred to the glories of the medieval Cambodian past, advocated a policy of complete self-sufficiency from what they called "year zero." There would not only be no exports and imports, but money and internal trade would be banned. "We won't use money again," stated one party document, "and

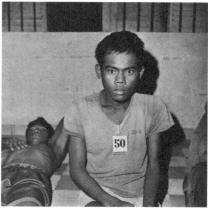

Prisoners from the Khmer Rouge's notorious Tuol Sleng prison in the capital of Phnom Penh: Chan Kim Srung (left), wife of foreign affairs minister Puk Suvann, with her child, and (right) an unidentified prisoner. The victims were photographed on arriving at the prison, before they were forced to "confess" to their crimes to their interrogators and stripped of their possessions. It is unlikely that the depicted survived the tortures of the prison. Tuol Sleng Genocide Museum

[we] will never ever think about re-circulating currency any more."[41] The educated "new people"—those Cambodians who had been tied into the money economy, legal thinking, modern technology and communications, and awareness of the outside world—were "infected" by their pasts, in contrast to the purity of the long-term village peasantry. The very "consciousness of private property," noted one party document, "is an enemy of the revolution."[42]

The Khmer Rouge government knew that the "new people" would suffer and die in the village labor camps to which they were sent. Of course, there was no mention that Pol Pot and a significant number of the party's leaders came from middle-class families and had been educated in Paris. But that did not seem to make any difference to their paranoid allegations against all teachers, businessmen, journalists, writers, doctors, nurses, accountants, and lawyers—really anyone who was educated and had had any contact with Western ways. In fact, anyone who wore glasses was immediately suspected, since they were readers and thinkers. These people—the "intellectuals"—were either killed immediately or sent off with their families to labor camps in the villages to work and often to die. During the four plus years of Khmer Rouge rule, regular schools were closed down and used for fertilizer warehouses. Libraries were shuttered and rare books were burned. The universities and their faculties were not allowed to function.[43] In identifying various gangs of opponents in the Northern Zone in the beginning of 1977, a Khmer Rouge official noted that most of the gangs had already been wiped out. The "fifth gang, made up of intellectuals, students, monks, teachers, and people who worked for the old regime, [is] almost wiped out."[44]

Those Cambodians who were sent off to the countryside for hard labor and reeducation endured cruel punishments, harsh labor conditions, and severe shortages of food. Generations of families were taken together to camps, where they were subordinated to "wholesome" village officials. Sometimes the children were sent off to separate camps for indoctrination in preparation for joining the army. One witness at the trial of Pol Pot and Ieng Sary testified: "After April 17, 1975 [the fall of Phnom Penh], they made my family go to the village of Cham Roa, in Mong Russey district, Battambang province. There were 48 members in my family, and only my son survived. All the others died from disease or starvation."[45]

The village internees suffered an appalling death as a result of hunger and disease brought on by a lack of food and nutrition. One survivor of the Cambodian genocide, whose family of "new people" had been sent to the villages as forced labor, draws a picture that would fit, as well, rural Ukraine, or the Chinese villages during the Great Leap Forward:

> Passing through the village, the stench of rotten flesh and human waste hangs heavily in the air. Many of the villagers are getting sicker and sicker from disease and starvation. They lie in their huts, whole families together, unable to move. Concave faces have the appearance of what they will look like once the flesh rots away. Other faces are swollen, waxy, and bloated, resembling a fat Buddha, except they don't smile. Their arms and legs are mere bones with fleshless fingers and toes attached to them. They lie there, as if no longer of this world, so weak they cannot swat away the flies sitting on their faces. Occasionally, parts of their bodies convulse involuntarily and you know they are alive. However, there is nothing we can do except let them lie there until they die.[46]

Many hundreds of thousands perished in this way. The Khmer Rouge insisted that the indigenous farmers in the countryside knew enough folk medicine to deal with problems of widespread disease. There was no real need, the Khmer leaders stated, for tainted Western medicine or Western pharmaceuticals, which were unavailable in any case. As a result, many more died of disease than would have been the case otherwise.

Not only were the Khmer Rouge mortally suspicious of anyone possibly influenced by the West, they also had a deep, paranoid fear of Vietnamese and Russian influence. The indigenous Vietnamese population of Cambodia, some 175,000 altogether, was considered both "racially" suspect and politically unreliable, since they could putatively be manipulated by Hanoi. Among the first planks of the Khmer Rouge program was to "expel the entire Vietnamese ethnic population."[47] By September 1975, as many as 150,000 Vietnamese had been expelled from the country, and many of them were killed along the way. As relations with Hanoi grew worse, the remaining Vietnamese were not allowed to leave, and the Khmer Rouge turned to mass killing. Husbands were ordered to kill their Vietnamese wives, and if they refused were themselves executed. Local officials were ordered to arrest all ethnic Vietnamese, as well as Khmers who spoke Vietnamese or who had Vietnamese friends. There were also massacres of Vietnamese, the largest of which was the mass execution of some 420 Vietnamese men, women, and children in Kompong Chhnang province in May 1977.[48] Those Vietnamese who were not killed outright were sent to insufficiently provisioned work camps where few survived.

The Angkor government also moved against and wiped out very large numbers of the Cambodian Cham population, a distinct Muslim people estimated at approximately 250,000. The Cham were concentrated in some seventy or so villages located mostly in the east of the country, along the Mekong River and its branches.[49] In their attempts to create a fully equal and nonhierarchical collective society, the Khmer Rouge attacked any group or people that stood out from the masses. The Cham, who insisted on their unique identity, customs, and religion, quickly became an object for elimination. Like the Vietnamese, the Cham were deported to labor camps, where large numbers of them died. They were forced to debase their own religion and renounce Allah. The Khmer Rouge insisted that the women cut their hair, instead of keeping it long in Cham style, and cease to wear their distinctive sarongs. They were forced to stop speaking their language and teaching their customs. They had to eat in communal dining rooms, where none of the prohibitions against pork were observed. Of course, as one survivor noted: "In fact, we never saw pork, but it was an excuse for the Khmer Rouge to kill people who said they would not eat it."[50] The Cham were targeted for elimination.

> There was no policy of [allowing] minority nationalities. Everyone was mixed together. There was only one race—the Khmer ... from liberation in 1975.... Pol Pot did not trust the Muslims. After 1975, in the eyes of the state organization there were no Muslims at all.[51]

The Khmer Rouge also forced other nationalities to give up their distinct cultures or face death: Thai, Lao, Chinese, Cambodian Catholics, and so on. A large percentage of these groups were killed: 50 percent of the Chinese, 40 percent of the Lao, 40 percent of the Thai, and 36 percent of the Cham—more than 300,000 people altogether.[52] There would be one undifferentiated mass of workers—traditional Khmer peasants and workers—led by the party center.

The Khmer Rouge not only destroyed the religious life of the minorities, they attacked the dominant Buddhist faith of Cambodia. The official stance was uncompromising: "Buddhism is a politically reactionary religion to be eliminated. Buddhist monks do nothing but eat and sleep and have exploited the population for more than 2,000 years. They are leeches sucking the people's blood." The regime ordered the monks to "shed their robes, [and] quit their religious life to go back to a secular life. Those who refused to comply were to be considered enemies and sent off to the nether world."[53] The Buddhist temples were pillaged, while the monks had to swear allegiance to the new way or be killed or sent to work in the mines. Many committed suicide; others tried to disguise themselves and survive in the jungles.[54] Only three thousand monks survived the Pol Pot regime, out of an original fifty thousand or more.

Like their Soviet and Chinese counterparts, the Khmer Rouge sought and found enemies inside the Communist Party. Once Pol Pot felt his regime was secure from enemies from the former regime and ethnic and religious aliens, he turned to eliminating internal foes. "Our enemies are now weakening and are going to die," stated a Foreign Ministry official, most probably the minister Ieng Sary, in January 1977.

> The revolution has pulled out their roots, and the espionage networks have been smashed; in terms of classes, our enemies are all gone. However, they still have the American imperialists, the revisionists, the KGB, and Vietnam. Though they have been defeated, they still go on. Another thing is that the enemies are on our body, among the military, the workers, in the cooperatives and even in our ranks. To make Socialist Revolution deeply and strongly, these enemies must be progressively wiped out.[55]

The party carried out a series of internal purges that enveloped especially those who had been involved with the Vietnamese and allegedly still sympathized with them. "The enemy must be crushed," Cambodian radio broadcasts beamed. "What is infected must be cut out." "What is too long must be shortened and made the right length."[56]

In communist genocides, revolutionary governments led by dictatorial leaders reified groups of alleged class and political enemies, and eliminated them as groups. The perpetrators often gave these opponents the characteristics frequently attributed to ethnic, religious, and national groups, and then eliminated them, in the words of the genocide convention, "as such." Often in the minds of the perpetrators, the categories of class and politics, on the one hand, and ethnic, religious, and national, on the other, overlapped, making it even more difficult to separate one kind of mass killing from another. The arguments about whether the Cham were killed as an ethnicity or as "Islamic Khmer," which the regime preferred to call them, or whether the Ukrainian peasants were starved to death because they were Ukrainians or peasants, are less relevant to the meaning of genocide than whether the respective regimes targeted and worked to eliminate these categories of human beings.

CHAPTER 7

Anti-Communist Genocides

T he Cold War introduced the element of global rivalry into the history of genocide and mass killing. The new bipolar world after World War II, dominated by the Soviet Union and the United States, set a context for genocide that often saw communist systems engaged in killing that was justified as the struggle against capitalism, whether as internal remnants of a supposed capitalist past or as external enemies. (Stalin's genocides fit this model, as well.) An analogous situation prevailed in some right-wing dictatorships after 1945, where genocide was imbued with the rhetoric and realities of internal threats by communist insurgencies or external incursions by communist powers. In both cases, the threats of the ideological opponents were misrepresented and blown out of proportion. More often than not, the alleged threats were used to accomplish aims that were otherwise unattainable. Leftists of various stripes, including some social democrats, were painted with the communist brush to defend their murder. This does not mean that Moscow (or Beijing and Havana) was not often involved in challenging anti-communist governments or that the United States did not encourage anti-communists to strike at alleged communist insurgencies.

Most of the anti-communist genocides took place during a period of intense rivalry in the Third World between the Soviet Union and the United States after the death of Stalin, who was little interested in a worldwide conflict with the Americans. Stalin's successors in the Kremlin—Nikita Khrushchev and Leonid Brezhnev—thought differently about the rivalry with the United States. The United States became an interventionist power, whereas the Soviet Union, aided by Cuba, in particular, supported revolutionary insurgencies when opportune. Genocide arose primarily from particularistic local politics and rivalries, but it drew much of its rhetorical context and ferocity from the Cold War.

The genocide in Guatemala had deep roots in the Cold War and its effects on Central America. After World War II, for the first time in Guatemalan history, a series of leftist-oriented governments stressed the importance of social and economic justice, condemning, in particular, the United Fruit Company for its colonialist attitudes toward the country, its resources, and its people. Leftists in and out of the government also increasingly focused on the widespread influence of U.S. neo-colonialism in the country, while pressing forward with nationalist platforms of development. Officials in Washington were not at all pleased when, in 1953 and 1954, the newly elected Guatemalan president, Jacobo Árbenz Guzmán, legalized the Communist Party and openly solicited its cooperation in programs of land reform and the nationalization of foreign companies, most prominently United Fruit. In Operation PBSUCCESS, President Dwight D. Eisenhower authorized the CIA to train and organize Guatemalan opposition military units in Honduras, a neighboring military dictatorship friendly to Washington. The $2.7 million budget allocated to the CIA for this purpose was to go for "psychological warfare and political action," as well as "subversion." In the process of planning the coup, the CIA drew up a list of "top-flight communists" to be eliminated by the new government.[1]

Inspired by the attention and support of Washington, the well-armed Guatemalan forces in Honduras, with right-wing Colonel Carlos Castillo Armas in command, invaded Guatemala and sought support from the Guatemalan army. The CIA's successful disinformation campaign that painted Árbenz as a communist and the air cover provided by the Americans for the right-wing campaign disheartened the Guatemalan president, who resigned without a fight on June 27, 1954. The Guatemalan military coup both energized the forces of the Latin American left (Che Guevara was in Guatemala City at the time of the coup and attributed his radicalization to this experience) and bolstered the confidence of right-wing military dictatorships in the region. Seen as an American policy success, the Guatemalan coup established a pattern of U.S. policy in Central and South America that was to persist for decades to come.

Under a series of right-wing military dictators in the 1950s and early 1960s, military officers, conservative landowners, business leaders, and the church establishment placed Guatemala in a social deepfreeze, where the vast majority of the population—the indigenous Mayans, mestizos, and Ladino campesinos—were condemned to a life of extreme poverty, unemployment, and even forced labor. Colonel Castillo and his forces arrested and in some cases executed Árbenz's supporters, beginning a cycle of violence that continued for over three decades. We are still unsure whether the killings of alleged communists that Castillo's government organized took their inspiration from the CIA's lists assembled before the coup.[2]

In the early 1960s, discontented younger Guatemalans joined with leftists and labor activists to form an insurgency in the eastern part of the country. The government, advised by the CIA and U.S. Special Forces, launched extensive counterinsurgency campaigns, which based their "scorched earth" policies on American tactics in Vietnam. For the first time in Guatemala, the military campaigns were accompanied by notable cases of people being kidnapped, tortured, killed, and "disappeared" by the Guatemalan security forces. As the counterinsurgency intensified, so did the massacres of innocent civilians and the destruction of villages seen as part of the support system of the rebels. Special semilegal units from the army and police operated as death squads, assassinating opponents of the regime and intimidating their families. These were supervised by the "Special Commando Unit," formed in January 1967, which carried out "abductions, bombings, street assassinations, and executions of real and alleged communists ... and other vaguely defined 'enemies of government.' "[3] The later Commission on Historical Clarification insisted that in this period "extreme cruelty was a resource used intentionally to produce and maintain a climate of terror in the population." The idea was "to intimidate and silence society as a whole, in order to destroy the will for transformation"[4]

The March 1978 election of Fernando Romeo Lucas García intensified the violence, as lines hardened between the army rulers and Indian opponents of the regime. In the notable "Panzós Massacre" of May 29, 1978, the Special Forces opened fire on a peaceful labor demonstration of some 700 Kekchi native mine workers and their families, killing an estimated 150 men, women, and children. In January 1980, a group of Indian peasants, protesting their forced eviction from lands that were given over to oil companies for exploration, moved into the Spanish embassy in Guatemala City. The police attacked with incendiary devices, killing thirty-six people, setting off another wave of protests. All in all, thousands of political opponents and opposition leaders were killed or "disappeared" in the period from 1978 to 1980. Amnesty International stated that more than 30,000 people were "abducted, tortured and assassinated" between 1966 and 1981.[5]

Peaceful change, labor protests, and democratic organization were impossible given the violent tactics of the government and military. The Mayan Quiché region became a major center of the insurgent movement led by the leftist Army of the Poor (EGP). The EGP had grown from a tiny group of just over a dozen men in 1972 to some five thousand fighters and ten thousand local irregulars in 1982.[6] The Cubans were active supporters, providing logistical advice and training.[7] Encouraged by the victories of the Sandinistas against the regime of Anastasio Somoza in neighboring Nicaragua, the insurgents mounted a major offensive in early 1981, which at times resembled a full-scale civil war, drawing in as many as a half a million supporters from the indigenous communities.

The counterinsurgency campaign mounted by the government was extreme and brutal; a series of terrible massacres demonstrated the readiness of the military to kill innocent civilians, especially of Mayan background. The leftist insurgents fought back, often committing atrocities and engaging in assassinations and retaliation of their own, though the number of their victims was dwarfed by the death toll exacted by the government. The brutal counterinsurgency morphed into genocide in the period 1981–1983.

With the unrestricted support of the Reagan administration, the Guatemalan Army launched Operation Ashes (Ceniza), which lasted from mid-1981 to the spring of 1982, an effective scorched-earth campaign aimed at depriving the insurgents of their rural base, especially in Quiché and Huehuetenango provinces. The death toll from the operation was unprecedented in Guatemala; as many as 35,000 people were reported to have been killed, the vast majority civilians.[8] A February 1992 CIA report noted that there was "well-documented belief" among the army that "the entire Ixil Indian population" sided with the insurgents, thus unit commanders of the operations were "instructed to destroy all the towns and villages which are cooperating with the guerilla army of the poor (EGP) and eliminate all sources of resistance."[9] This meant that all Mayans, including women and children, were designated as enemies and potentially targeted for destruction. The army burned Mayan villages to the ground, destroying the peasants' animals and fields so no one would return.

This campaign was only a prelude to the start of the second stage of the military counterinsurgency, which can be dated to the March 23, 1982, coup d'état of General Efraín Ríos Montt, who was convicted of genocide in Guatemala in 2013, but subsequently released. Soon after assuming office, the general and his advisers in part abandoned the indiscriminant violence of Operation Ashes because it tended to drive the Mayan peoples deeper into the mountains or into border areas of Mexico. Instead, Ríos Montt, advertised by Washington as a thoroughgoing democrat and born-again Christian, undertook a series of targeted operations to destroy the Mayan resistance—indeed, to destroy the Mayans themselves as an independent people. His plans, "Operation Sofia" and "Victoria 82," outlined a strategy of superimposing onto the campaigns of wanton destruction an effort to separate the Mayan people from the insurgents, by offering them incentives to relocate to "strategic villages," which were maintained and run by the army.[10] This so-called guns-and-beans policy, initiated in July of 1982, proved to be little more than an attempt to deprive the Mayans of their autonomy and destroy their ability to resist.

The violence of the army and police units was unprecedented, even for the already brutal two decades of the civil war. The commanders were given carte blanche to destroy the insurgents and their active supporters. Those who escaped into the mountains were bombarded by air. The scorched-earth policy left wide swaths of the fertile countryside in flames. ("We have no scorched-earth policy," Ríos Montt insisted, after a meeting with Ronald Reagan. "We have a policy of scorched communists."[11]) Villages were razed to the ground. If villages and fields were abandoned, the soldiers destroyed them as well, since this meant that the former inhabitants supported the insurgents. Much of the violence was directed against women and children. Women were raped individually and in groups, most certainly as a way to degrade and destroy the Mayans as a people. Children were killed as *delinquentes subservios*, or potential subversives.[12] The testimonies of victims provided to the Spanish Federal Court in February 2008 leave a heartrending trail of stories of woe. One witness recalled that she had returned to the village after the initial incursions by the soldiers:

> There were people outside their houses crying. When we arrived in the center, I saw a huge pile of ashes and cinders, a pile of bodies, half of them still burning.... The square was full of blood. I saw bullet shells scattered everywhere. We went back to my house again to get containers of water to try to put of [out] the fire.... It continued to burn and the smell of the poor people burning was like burned chicken feathers.

After encountering a number of survivors slowly walking along the path with torn clothes and distracted looks, she asked one of her neighbors what had happened:

> She just looked at me and did not speak, because they had cut off her lips. This poor woman had been raped. She had no skirt, so I put a skirt on her and offered her water. She was like a child.

Her testimony concluded with descriptions of corpses strewn alongside the path, some partly eaten by dogs.[13]

The Commission on Historical Clarification summarized the terrible violence against the Mayans as follows:

> In the majority of massacres there is evidence of multiple acts of savagery, which preceded, accompanied or occurred after the deaths of victims. Acts such as killing of defenseless children, often by beating them against walls or throwing them alive into pits where the corpses of adults were later thrown; the amputation of limbs; the impaling of victims; the killing of persons by covering them in petrol and burning them alive; the extraction, in the presence of others, of the viscera of the victims who were still alive; the confinement of people who had been mortally tortured, in agony for days; the opening of wombs of pregnant women, and other similarly atrocious acts.[14]

Seventy-five thousand people were killed in the most awful ways within eighteen months, most in the first eight months of the campaign. It has been estimated that in the Ixil triangle a third of the local population was killed.[15]

The attempt to set up "strategic villages"—the "beans" part of the guns-and-beans strategy—also ended in violence, as recruits of military age were dragooned into the army, forced to serve in civilian detachments, and sometimes tortured and killed if they were deemed suspicious. The army also closely regulated and controlled the life of the villages. There were strict rules about how much food one could consume, what clothes the residents could wear, and when the people could leave their homes. The Mayans were not allowed to wear their traditional dress, engage in Mayan cultural activities, or celebrate their holidays.[16] Their sacred places were destroyed and ceremonial life prohibited. According to "Victoria 82," political meetings were banned except for those supervised by the military. There was strict military control over the storage and distribution of food and medical supplies. The military also strictly controlled movement by issuing papers and routinely checking those papers at guard posts in towns and on the roads.[17]

This two-pronged strategy by Ríos Montt included the shadowy activities of secret death squads, which targeted labor leaders, university students, educators, Mayan activists, and other opponents of the government. Right-wing death squads were responsible for an increasing number of dead bodies showing up "in ditches and gullies," which the U.S. ambassador noted were "executions ordered by armed services officers close to President Ríos Montt."[18] Although Ríos Montt himself was removed in a coup of August 8, 1983, the activities of the death squads continued well into the decade. The feared group "El Archivo" kept a "death squad diary" from 1983 to 1985, which was subsequently discovered by researchers.[19] The incidence of massacres decreased markedly as the military established control over the Mayan territories and the insurgents either fled deeper into the mountains or into Mexico. Only the peace process begun in the mid-1990s finally brought the protracted civil war to an end.

The Commission on Clarification, part of the peace process, concluded that the Guatemalan government committed genocide against the Mayans, attacking them as inherently suspect politically and as an enemy nation. It sought to deprive the indigenous peoples of their culture and their way of life. The state was responsible for 93 percent of the killing, most of that by the military. The guerrillas were responsible only for 3 percent of the fatalities in the civil war. In other words, this was a civil war only in name; what happened was a case of serial massacres organized by the army and paramilitary, especially of the Mayan in El Quiché, where 344 documented cases took place. The goal of the perpetrators "was to kill the largest number of group members possible," including women and children. These massacres were not random, but in the Commission's language, they "obeyed a higher, strategically planned policy, manifested in actions which had a logical and coherent sequence."[20] Some 200,000 people lost their lives in the Guatemalan civil war; another million or more were displaced.

At roughly the same time as the beginning of the Guatemalan civil war—and in a similar if distinctly Asian Cold War context—the Indonesian military, supported by its allies in society, most notably Islamist political movements, attacked the PKI, the Communist Party of Indonesia, in 1965 and 1966, destroying its organization, and in a frenzy of anti-communist fervor, killing at the least 500,000 Indonesian men, women, and children. Unlike in Guatemala, there was little race hatred involved. The Indonesian military and militias did attack Chinese civilians, as well as Chinese members of the PKI, because of the alleged ties between the Indonesian communists and the Chinese Communist Party. These attacks were related to the resentment and racism many Indonesians felt toward Chinese merchants. But in Indonesia, both the attackers and the attacked were mostly Muslims, who made up about 90 percent of the country's population. "Anti-communist" meant something different in the context of Indonesia from what it did in Guatemala. There was much less ideological hostility in Indonesia to communism per se than there was to the PKI as a rival political organization to the army.[21] In fact, the basis of President Sukarno's rule—what he called "guided democracy"—was the generally popular idea of "Nasakom": Nationalism, Religion, and Communism.

There is much that remains unknown about the reasons for the genocidal killings of the Indonesian communists. Unquestionably, there were tensions between the army and the PKI that could be traced back to the struggle against the Dutch in the war of independence (1945–1949), when communist influence in the army was strong and professional soldiers resented the politicization of the military by the communists.[22] Islamists also resented the PKI's influence, which they worried would lead to a militantly secular regime in Jakarta. Sukarno was still widely respected by his countrymen as a symbol of the anti-colonialist struggle for independence, and as an opponent of American aims in Southeast Asia. But tensions had grown between the government and the army because of Sukarno's increasing flirtation with the Chinese communists and his reliance on the PKI and some well-known communist sympathizers for governing the country. PKI support for land reform, especially in East Java, antagonized Muslim landowners and clerics, with whom the army was allied. With some 300,000 dedicated leadership cadres and around 2 million members altogether, the PKI was a formidable force. It was the third largest communist party in the world and the largest in any non-communist country. There was good reason for PKI opponents to be concerned about a situation in which Sukarno would become completely captive to communist aims.

But these kinds of tensions within societies do not necessarily lead to genocide. The interests of political leaders are usually involved, and Indonesia was no exception. The primary movers behind the chain of events that led to genocide still remain hidden behind the murky curtain of transition from the Sukarno to the Suharto regime that took place in late 1965 and early 1966. Unlike in Guatemala, the Americans in Indonesia were confined to being discreet cheerleaders on the sidelines of the suppression of the PKI. State Department officials admitted at the time that relations between the United States and Indonesia "have been poisoned by a sea of hatred" and that the United States "has been too firmly established as the enemy of Indonesian national hopes and ambitions" to exert any serious influence on the course of events.[23]

What we do know is that on the night and morning of September 30–October 1, 1965, Lt. Colonel Untung led a group of young officers from the Palace Guard, subsequently called the September 30 Movement, which seized and executed six generals, most of them known as right-wing anti-communists. General Suharto, who was one of the leading figures in the army and an uneasy confederate of Sukarno's, took charge of the army and proclaimed that the conspiracy against the state had been defeated, and that he and the army were in firm control of Jakarta. Sukarno himself might well have been involved in the September 30 plot as a way to bolster his power by increasing the number of pro-PKI figures in the army leadership.[24] It is probable that a narrow clique of the clandestine bureau of the PKI was implicated in the plot.[25] In any case, Sukarno quickly distanced himself from the coup attempt, but was outflanked by Suharto, who proceeded to oversee a broad and effective propaganda campaign to blame the PKI and the communists for killing and allegedly mutilating the generals, badly wounding the young daughter of another general—who became a cause célèbre—and for trying to seize control of the government.

Rumors were planted that members of the communist-allied Indonesian Women's Movement, the Gerwani, did naked dances around the dead generals' corpses before castrating them and engaging in an orgy with the conspirators.[26] These kinds of highly inflammatory rumors about the PKI and the Gerwani spread quickly all over Indonesia. The activist women were portrayed as communist seductresses, who would use sex to kill, maim, and castrate members of the army and police.[27]

The coup was almost too good to be true for the conservative generals, who had grown increasingly uneasy about the PKI's power and its alliance with Sukarno.[28] Now, Suharto led a broad attack on the party, arresting its leading cadres in Jakarta and destroying its bases of operations. Army leaders organized demonstrations in the capital, while army-sponsored youth groups wreaked havoc on local communists and their supporters. The nationalist party, the PNI, and its militant youth groups were also involved. Eventually, the army caught up with the chairman of the PKI, Aidit, along with a number of other party leaders, in Central Java. They were all arrested in conjunction with the September 30 movement and executed. Aidit himself may or may not have been involved in the original coup attempt.

The army's open attack on one of the three pillars of Sukarno's rule, communism, encouraged a variety of opponents of the PKI to join the fray. Meanwhile, the anti-communist rhetoric in the press and on television inflamed local opinion against PKI adherents.[29] Indonesia is a highly diverse society, perhaps better described as a number of societies, spread out across the vast archipelago that makes up its territory. The PKI had made enemies in a variety of regions, ranging from Aceh, where the predominantly conservative Islamic rulers and population despised the communists, to mostly Hindi Bali, where the intricacies of the caste system often found the PKI and its allies opposed by the upper-caste rulers of much of the island. In Bali, even the caste distinctions did not always determine who would be killed.[30]

Straightforward social or religious explanations for mass killing are often too easy for situations where local resentments between (even within) families, clans, and other micro-communities could be expressed within the violent context of the anti-PKI campaign. In particularly tense situations, some people joined the killing who might have felt that by standing back they could be accused of being a communist themselves, which often happened. While spontaneous pogroms did take place, on the whole, the killing of communists happened only after army units had been dispatched to the various localities. In Bali, the regional military commander ordered a full-scale assault on the PKI only when it became clear that this was in conformance with attacks in other regions.[31] Army units sometimes got involved in the arrests and killing of communists themselves. But most often they provided legitimation and a framework for the massacres and executions through their sheer presence, and by training and arming local vigilantes to search out and destroy PKI organizations and members. Sometimes it was enough that they provided the transportation for gangs of killers. A Dutch journalist reported from Bali:

> Riding in police trucks, the military Balinese entered villages where communists lived. The communists were rounded up and taken by truck to another village where they were slaughtered with knives [klewang] or shot dead in police prisons. To prevent later acts of revenge, in most cases the entire family or even the extended family were killed.[32]

The army often showed up in the regions with lists of targeted PKI members, while in others, they collected lists as they went. There remains some controversy about the role of the U.S. Embassy in supplying the Indonesian military with the names of 5,000 of the leading communist cadres. There is no question that the lists were supplied to the army; the issue is whether those lists made a substantial difference to the success of the killing. The Americans were certainly aware of what was happening all over the archipelago. On October 29, the Embassy reported: "Moslem fervor in Atjeh [Aceh] apparently put all but a few PKI out of action. Atjehnese have decapitated PKI and placed their heads on stakes along the road. Bodies of PKI victims reportedly thrown into rivers or sea as Atjehnese refused [to] 'contaminate' soil." On November 8, the Embassy noted that there were "wholesale killings" in northern Sumatra and Aceh. A local police chief in Central and East Java told the U.S. officials that "100–150 PKI members were being killed every night by civilian anti-Communist troops with blessing of the Army." In Surabaya, the capital of East

Java, a missionary informed them that 3,500 PKI members were killed between November 4 and 9 in Kediri and 200 in nearby Paree. Reports came in that in Central Javi PKI adherents were "shot on sight" by the army. The Embassy noted that the death toll in Bali was 80,000, with "no end in sight." "We frankly do not know whether the real figure is closer to 100,000 or 1,000,000," wrote the Embassy, "but believe it is wiser to err on the side of the lower estimates, especially when questioned by the press."[33]

The relatively few extant eyewitness accounts of the killing make it clear that wide swaths of Indonesian society experienced the terror, not just the targeted PKI members and their families.[34] All the reporters mention the rise of "tensions" and the fear that pervaded towns and villages of Indonesia, backwater villages, as well as more prominent cities. Rioters looted Chinese merchants, killing many and kidnapping others for ransom in the process. PKI installations and headquarters were burned down. Anyone who tried to protect the party's property was killed. Nationalist and Muslim youth groups attacked their own particular enemies, while the police stood aside when they did not actively abet the killing. The predominantly young assailants assumed poses of matinee martial arts heroes, looking to test their mettle and commitment by acts of killing. Some Christians fell victim to the Muslim vigilantes; in other cases, Christians joined the gangs of killers. In Bali, the killers were mostly Hindu nationalists, who were told by their leaders that the PKI were enemies of religion and "must be eliminated and destroyed down to the roots."[35]

Local groups of vigilantes, often accompanied by designated killers, sometimes very young and politically naïve, sometimes older and more "professional" in their executioner's art, would slice off peoples' heads and body parts, collecting the heads in bags as some kind of trophy collection. Sometimes, just the entrails of the victims were left for the relatives, while the bodies were dumped elsewhere. As one witness wrote, the rivers were swollen with corpses:

> And usually, the corpses were no longer recognizable as human. Headless. Stomachs torn open. The smell was unbelievable. To make sure they didn't sink, the carcasses were deliberately tied to, or impaled on, bamboo stakes. And the departure of corpses from the Kediri region down the Brantas achieved its golden age when bodies were stacked together on rafts over which the PKI banner proudly flew.[36]

The severing and then displaying of body parts, in addition to sowing terror and fear in local population, also made proper burial impossible, which in many of the cultures of Indonesia was a way to undermine the dignity and sense of self of the enemy.

The perpetrators were the same in the cases of the genocide of the Indonesian communists and in the case of East Timor: General Suharto, the Indonesian military, and government militia groups. The justification behind the killing was similar: the need to fight the evil of communism and destroy its traitorous, and in the case of East Timor, secessionist potential. Otherwise, the campaigns were different. In fact, the genocide in East Timor resembled much more the case of Guatemala than that of the Indonesian communists. Genocide in East Timor took place over a long period of time, from 1975, when the Indonesian army invaded the island, until late 1999, when an Australian-led international force, endorsed by the United Nations, took over East Timor from the Indonesians, with East Timorese independence to follow in 2002. Although the suffering and death that made up the East Timor genocide was protracted, eliminating roughly 25 percent of the East Timorese population of 650,000, as in the case of Guatemala it had its peaks and troughs, with by far the largest number of people, some 100,000 altogether, dying in the period 1977–1979.[37]

The central thrust of the genocidal campaign in East Timor, as in Guatemala, is hard to separate analytically from the counterinsurgency tactics that exceeded all boundaries of the necessary. Rape, torture, massacres, the burning of villages and the destruction of crops, with the resulting famine—all were part of the experiences of the East Timorese and the Guatemalans. In both places, the respective armies set up "strategic hamlets" to separate the civilian population from the insurgents and transit camps to "filter" the population for communists and communist sympathizers. The perpetrators in East Timor were mostly Javanese Muslims—in fact, the East Timorese called the Indonesians simply Javanese—while the victims were almost all Roman Catholic Timorese (East Timor was approximately 90 percent Catholic at the time), who are themselves a polyglot mixture of some thirty indigenous and immigrant peoples.[38] But the real motivation behind the genocide in East Timor was neither religious nor ethnic, though both markers of Timorese identity played a role in the persecutions.[39] Jakarta was intent on absorbing East Timor into Indonesia and forcing its population to accept Suharto's "New Order"—a consensus community ruled and represented by the Indonesian army. In that sense, the Indonesians sought to crush the East Timorese as a "national" group with national aspirations, though there were plenty of Timorese who sided with the Indonesian program.

The immediate backdrop to the crisis in East Timor was the precipitous decline of Portugal's will to maintain its crumbling colonial empire, including East Timor. With problems enough at home and severe challenges in Africa, Portugal was ready in the early 1970s to allow East Timor its independence. The East Timorese formed themselves into a series of political parties to influence the course of events. The most powerful of these parties was Fretilin (the Revolutionary Front for an Independent East Timor), a left-wing party comprising mostly social democrats, though with some communists involved. The UDT (the Timorese Democratic Union) was made up mostly of the former colonial elite of East Timor and favored a slow evolution toward independence and some form of continued association with Portugal. The third important party was the Apodete (the Timorese Popular Democratic Association), which advocated union with Indonesia and was used by the Indonesians for their own policy goals in the intense political struggle within East Timor.

By focusing on Fretilin's communist sympathies, Jakarta was successful in driving a wedge between Fretilin and the UDT to the point where the UDT staged a coup in mid-August 1975 in anticipation of Portuguese withdrawal, setting off a civil war with Fretilin. But Fretilin

At a meeting at Camp David on July 5, 1975, President Gerald R. Ford (in light jacket) discussed the problems of the decolonization of East Timor with Indonesian President Suharto (to Ford's left). In the months leading up to the December 7, 1975, invasion, President Ford and Secretary of State Henry Kissinger (back to camera) went along with Suharto's intention to take control of the country.

had strong supporters within the former Timorese army that had served the Portuguese, and in a brief if fierce struggle that cost as many as 2,000 lives, managed to gain the upper hand and seize control of the capital of Dili.[40] With a combination of indifference and vacillation in the international community (and in Portugal) about the fate of East Timor, Fretilin declared the country's independence, hoping to stave off an Indonesian invasion and garner the protection of the U.N. But the party's actions served as a casus belli for Suharto and the Indonesian army, which invaded East Timor in 1975 and seized control of most of the nascent country, despite fierce Fretilin resistance.

With the tacit approval of the U.S. administration, the self-interested "realism" of the neighboring Australians, and the general approbation or indifference of the international community, the Indonesian military invaded East Timor in Operation Komodo (December 1975), attacking Fretilin's forces with frightening intensity. No holds were barred, as the Indonesians used advanced air weaponry, sea power, and artillery to destroy the East Timorese enemy. In operations known as "encirclement and destroy," they even employed chemical defoliants to flush out and eliminate their opponents.[41] From the very beginning of the invasion, Indonesian troops engaged in massacres. Timorese of all ages were mowed down in the capital of Dili as the army took control of the city, killing some 2,000 people altogether, including 700 Chinese. The killing spread to cities on the coast, where in some towns, it was reported that whole populations, save for infants, were killed.[42]

The counterinsurgency actions took on even more lethal dimensions when the Indonesians organized militias among the East Timorese, recruiting locals through force and sometimes through conviction. "Jorge," an East Timorese militia member who was recruited by the Indonesians while still in high school, later stated:

> We were warned; all who didn't join their army had to take the consequences. That means they say you are a Communist. None of us wanted to but there was no way not to fight. If you didn't fight you get killed yourself. I went on operations to kill other Timorese, ordinary people, then I felt strange. None of us felt good. At first we were sad, we have [sic] remorse, but after two or three years it was easy. You get used to killing.[43]

Fratricidal killing, then, went hand in hand with the operations of the Indonesian military. Much of the murderous activity during the occupation of East Timor can be attributed to Timorese themselves who were organized by the Indonesian army in militias and gangs.

Once it became clear that the Fretilin fighters, organized in a revolutionary military formation called Falintil, could fight to a stand-off with the Indonesian army and militias and were able to defend some "free zones" in the eastern highlands of the country, the policies of the Indonesians focused hard on separating the civilian population of the country from the "rebels." Whole village populations accused of harboring sympathies with Fretilin were forcibly removed to other—often less fertile—parts of the country along the coast and isolated from the highlands. With roughly 40,000 combat troops and militia in 1977–78, the army launched search-and-destroy missions that tried to confine the remainder of the East Timorese population in the mountains around the area of Mt. Matebian, where approximately thirty thousand people fought for their lives. The scene was described by Fretilin leader Xanana Gusmão:

> I visited all the front lines engaged in combat. There was no room for the people. There were bombardments, explosions, death, blood, smoke, dust, and interminable queues of people waiting for their turn to get a bit of water for the children.... There was total lack of control.... The fighter planes were sowing the seeds of death all day long.[44]

Other Fretilin-controlled villages were also bombed and strafed. Many were torched and food stores taken or destroyed. The Indonesian soldiers laid waste to the countryside and persecuted, killed, kidnapped, tortured, and raped along the way.

Those civilians who joined the insurrection with Fretilin suffered terribly from hunger and disease, and began to surrender in large numbers to the Indonesians, who put them in so-called transit camps, where they were interrogated, tortured, and sometimes killed. Collaborationist Apodete spies were used by the Indonesians to ferret out the Fretilin and Falintil members in the camps for "special treatment." Informants sometimes settled private quarrels by accusing fellow Timorese of being communists. The conditions of internment were dreadful; the Timorese often had no shelter at all except for trees; sanitation standards were ignored; as food supplies were minimal, people began to starve. The destruction wrought in the countryside by the army induced a terrible famine. East Timor was engulfed by malnutrition and by the diseases—dysentery, edema, diarrhea, and cholera—that accompanied it. Many tens of thousands died as a result.

The army sent those Timorese who made it through the transit camps to one hundred or so settlements, where the conditions were little better than in the transit camps. There was no real freedom of movement within the settlements, and it was almost impossible for the Timorese to plant and harvest crops. Instead, they sold their last valuables to corrupt army or militia members in exchange for bits of food. By 1979, the Indonesian army had confined as many as 300,000 to 370,000 Timorese in these settlements.[45] The idea of resettling so many people was in part to break up the social networks that supported the rebellion and to destroy family and clan solidarity, while importing Indonesians to take the place of demoralized and dying Timorese.[46] When a delegation of journalists was allowed to visit East Timor in early 1978, one described the resettlement camp in Remexio, which had already suffered a terrible massacre in the early days of the occupation:

> In Remexio as in most of the other towns, the people are stunned, sullen, and dispirited. Emaciated as a result of deprivation and hardship, they are struggling to make sense of the nightmarish interlude in which as much as half the population was uprooted.... The townspeople are undernourished and desperately in need of medical attention.[47]

By the end of the 1970s, the Indonesian army leaders were confident that their brutal counterinsurgency strategy had worked. Moreover, on December 31, 1978, they had managed to catch up with and kill Fretilin leader (and briefly in 1975, president of East Timor) Nicolau Lobato. In March 1979, the Indonesian government declared that East Timor had been "pacified."[48] Up to this point, the Indonesians, despite increasing pressure from the outside, would not allow relief missions into the country to deal with the terrible conditions of a huge number of Timorese. Finally, in October 1979, humanitarian aid began to filter into the country. Some 300,000 Timorese were said at this time to have been "seriously or critically malnourished."[49] Meanwhile, the Indonesians began a resettlement campaign of some 150,000 Indonesians with families to dilute the Timorese culture and reduce the pressure for independence. There were suggestions that this move, along with the ongoing systematic rape of Timorese women, was intended to "breed out" Timorese blood.[50]

Despite the humanitarian disaster among their compatriots, the Falintil managed to survive in small cells committed to undertaking selected guerilla actions against Indonesian army installations. As the attacks grew in the 1980s in particular, the Indonesian military overreacted by arresting suspected sympathizers, killing and "disappearing" supposed Falintil members and their supporters, and deporting families, often women and children, to Atauro. Fretilin had declared itself a "Marxist-Leninist party," which gave Suharto all the ammunition he needed to obtain sophisticated counterinsurgency equipment from the United States and to blunt criticism from Catholic human rights organizations, which were calling attention to the desperate plight of the Timorese population.

The Indonesians tried a variety of tactics to wipe out the remaining Falintil troops and capture their charismatic leader, Xanana Gusmão, who later became president and then prime minister of independent East Timor. In mid-1981, the army dragooned tens of thousands, some suggest as many as 145,000, Timorese men and boys to form a "fence of legs," which, backed up by 12,000 soldiers, was meant to flush out the guerillas from the bush. (One is reminded of the 1830 Tasmanian human chain, or "Black Line," to capture aborigines who had escaped the clutches of the local government.) In fact, the tactics did little else than damage agriculture further in a time of famine by taking so many farmers from their lands. The army seized a few women and old folks who were hiding in the bush.[51]

There were also a series of terrible massacres in the 1980s and early 1990s that highlighted the ongoing genocidal tactics of the Indonesians in East Timor. In August 1983, at Malim Luro on the southern coast, the Indonesians bound together a group of sixty Timorese, including many women and children, and bulldozed them to death.[52] In September, the villagers of Bibileo, who had fled the army's persecution, were exterminated in a series of massacres at Kraras, where fifty-five people ranging in age from one to sixty-one were forced into a hole in the earth and killed, and at Buikarin, where an estimated 141 men were separated from the women and executed. The women and children were sent on to Lalerek Mutin, an uninhabited area of Viqueque (Vikeke) district. The Catholic prelate Carlos Belo visited the region soon afterwards and reported to the governor of East Timor:

> I'm going to tell you something that you might not believe. I went to [Lalerek] Mutin. There weren't any men. Only women and children. There weren't any houses either. When the military took them to [Lalerek] Mutin, the military took all the villagers' possessions. They don't have houses—they're living in a field. They killed all the adult men, all of them. There are a few who ran into the forest. And they were all buried near the Luca river.[53]

The Santa Cruz Massacre of November 12, 1991, may be the best known of the army's excesses in this period because it was captured on video by a British filmmaker and circulated in the West. Approximately two thousand young people marched through the Timorese capital of Dili to the grave of a youth killed by the pro-Indonesian militia a week earlier. Indonesian soldiers surrounded the young people and, without giving any warning, opened fire on the demonstration. Some 270 young people were killed, many of them while in captivity in military trucks or even in hospitals afterwards.[54] There were rumors confirmed by numerous sources that the captured youth were beaten, stoned, injected with poison, and crushed under trucks.[55]

The situation in East Timor was on the agenda of human rights groups and Catholic activists throughout the 1990s, though with little concrete results, except for episodic famine relief. Timorese death squads, known as the "Ninjas" or "Bufo," worked together with the military in order to murder and "disappear" known or suspected supporters of independence. A Nelson Mandela–like figure, Gusmão was captured by the Indonesians in 1992 and placed in prison in Jakarta. The increasing international attention to the situation in East Timor, including a visit by the pope in 1989, meant that Gusmão would have to be kept alive. As a result, he continued to exercise influence on his followers. But even to the very end, when Suharto was forced to resign in May 1998, and the East Timorese voted in a referendum for independence in September 1999, with 78.5 percent of the population voting positively, the violence did not cease.

After twenty-four years of Indonesian misrule, the international community had seen enough. Deeply concerned that the mass killing of Timorese would spread, the United States and its allies cut off military aid to Jakarta. The United Nations authorized the deployment of a multinational force, led by the Australians, which convinced the Indonesians to withdraw their troops, call off their militias, and restore order to the country. On May 21, 2002, East Timor became an independent country, led predominantly by Fretilin members and Falintil veterans.

The East Timor situation highlights some of the general characteristics of anti-communist genocide. The victim group was predominantly defined in political terms. In East Timor, this was Fretilin, its members, their families, and its alleged supporters. As in the case of the Mayans in El Quiché, whole Timorese villages were implicated in what the perpetrators thought of as communities of opposition that were designated for complete destruction. This meant not only that innocent men, women, and children would die, as future generations of opponents, but also that their homes and fields would be destroyed. An Indonesian soldier was quoted as having said: "When you clean your field, don't you kill all the snakes, the small and large alike?"[56] The members of Fretilin, like those of the Guatemalan EGP and the communist PKI, along with their alleged sympathizers, were ascribed by the respective perpetrators with biological characteristics of lesser beings, who had to be eliminated altogether in order for the healthy new orders to survive and prosper.

CHAPTER 8

Genocide in the Post–Cold War World

Beginning in the mid-1990s, the publicity about the problems in East Timor contributed to the overall explosion of interest in and attention to the international crime of genocide. One can describe the past three decades as an era of human rights consciousness, human rights talk, and human rights action, focused in good measure on the global problems of genocide. The development of Holocaust consciousness in the 1970s and early 1980s—sparked by the 1961 trial of Adolf Eichmann and the 1967 Arab-Israeli war—undoubtedly contributed to an intellectual and emotional atmosphere that heightened sensitivities to genocide. But it was primarily the war in former Yugoslavia from 1991 to 1995, the Rwandan genocide in 1994, and the intervention in Kosovo in 1999 that brought genocide, a previously marginalized subject, to the attention of international society. These events, in turn, spawned even greater interest among nongovernmental organizations (NGOs) in human rights issues and prompted U.N., U.S., and European officials to set up special tribunals in the last half of the 1990s, the International Criminal Tribunal for Yugoslavia (ICTY) in The Hague and the International Criminal Tribunal for Rwanda (ICTR) in Arusha, Tanzania. The Rome Statute, agreed to in 1998 by 120 countries, set up the International Criminal Court (ICC), which came into existence in 2002 specifically to prosecute crimes against humanity, war crimes, and genocide.

Much of this activity on the human rights front was prompted by the tragic war in the former Yugoslavia. This multinational state, located in the western Balkans, disintegrated at the beginning of the 1990s with genocidal consequences. The intense involvement of the media and political figures in the West with the Yugoslav events brought considerable attention to the violence. Images of gaunt-faced internment camp inmates in the Balkans moved European and American publics to recognize that horrific crimes could occur again on the European continent on the eve of the twenty-first century. The complex problems that the West faced in dealing with the wars in the Balkans and the crimes that accompanied them—delaying substantive intervention until the late summer and early fall of 1995—recalled the earlier inept response of the West in the face of the Holocaust. The growing realization that the Rwandan genocide of 1994 could have been prevented with minimal effort, and that the U.N. and the United States had avoided engagement through bureaucratic stalling, heightened the awareness of the international community that genocide and crimes against humanity could and should be prevented. The principle that nations have an internationally recognized "Responsibility to Protect" their peoples against genocide and crimes against humanity took root at the end of the 1990s, after the successful intervention in Kosovo; the United Nations formally adopted the "Responsibility to Protect" at its 2005 world summit.

The death of Yugoslav communist boss Marshall Josip Broz Tito, in 1980, set off the spiral of events that ended up destroying the Yugoslav state. The failure of communist ideology and the socialist state to meet the complex challenges of running a multinational country with a stalled economy led in the 1980s to the explosive growth of nationalist ideologies among the component republics of the Yugoslav federation, each of which felt abused in its own way by the central government in Belgrade. Even Serb politicians increasingly complained that their national cause had been undermined by communist rule, turning to Serbian nationalism as the answer. Slobodan Milošević, a former communist banker, became the leader of the nationalist turn in Serbian politics. In Croatia, the historian Franjo Tuđman championed the cause of Croatian nationalism in the political arena, urging his compatriots to line up behind the nationalist (often fascist) symbols and program of Croat independence during the Second World War and find a way to escape from Belgrade's domination. In his own way, Alija Izetbegović, the Bosnian Muslim leader, also used Bosnian nationalist rhetoric to build the Party of Democratic Action, which he helped to found in 1989. But he was far from the "Islamic fundamentalist" portrayed by Croat and especially Serb critics.

Although the initial signs of serious conflict came from Slovenia in June of 1991, it was the war between Serbia and Croatia that broke out soon thereafter that contained the first portents of genocide. Unlike Slovenia, Croatia had a large minority of some 580,000 Serbs—12 percent of its population. They resided mostly in compact Serb communities in Krajina, a former border territory of the Austro-Hungarian Empire. As Tuđman's party, the HDZ (Croat Democratic Union), pushed the agenda of independence, the Croatian Serbs protested by setting up their own Republic of Serb Krajina, cleansing the region of Croats, and erecting armed barriers on the roads to Zagreb and the coast.

Facing an all-out Serbian attack on Vukovar in the eastern part of Croatia in late August 1991, the Croats organized their infant military, police, and militia groups to resist the Serbian militias and the Yugoslav army. Nevertheless, Vukovar fell to the Serbs on November 20, after three months of bombardment and bitter fighting. So many people were killed and so many buildings destroyed in the shelling that the city was turned into "the Hiroshima of our days," wrote one observer.[1] Behind the Serbian lines, Milošević proceeded with his plans to absorb occupied Croatian territories into a newly constituted, Serb-dominated Yugoslavia. Željko Ražnatović, known as Arkan, and his paramilitary gang, the Tigers, wreaked havoc among Croat civilians, robbing, threatening, killing, and raping.

The taking of Vukovar and the occupation of eastern Slavonia introduced the element of genocide into campaigns of ethnic cleansing. On

November 19, 1991, Yugoslav army soldiers and Serb paramilitary forces entered a local hospital in Vukovar. Most of the sick and wounded were evacuated to a "detention center" located at a nearby warehouse, where the prisoners were robbed and beaten. A number of the wounded were then transferred to a prison in Sremska Mitrovica. The next morning, according to the ICTY, Yugoslav army solders separated the women and children from the remaining men, many still on stretchers, and transported them from the detention center. Many of the men were tortured and beaten, two of them so badly that they died. One ICTY investigator later described a regular "orgy of beatings" in Vukovar.[2] Two hundred prisoners were then taken to the Ovčara farm outside of Vukovar, massacred, and buried in a mass grave.[3] It was the first, though certainly not the last, time in the war that ethnic cleansing was accompanied by what might be considered acts of genocide.

The events in Slovenia and Croatia affected the other peoples of the Yugoslav Federation, as well. The Macedonians, Montenegrins, Kosovar Albanians, and, most fatefully, the Bosnians, looked to advance their programs of independence, as the Serbs tried to hold together a Belgrade-dominated "Greater Serbia" within the crumbling borders of Yugoslavia. The inhabitants of Bosnia-Herzegovina were in the largest part Muslims (43 percent), but there were also substantial minorities of Serbs (31 percent) and of Croats (17 percent). Before the Serb-Croat war, Milošević and Tuđman had agreed to partition Bosnia between themselves, leaving a small rump portion around Sarajevo for the Muslims. Once Izetbegović's Muslim Party of Democratic Action expressed its intention to declare independence, both the Bosnian Serbs and the Croats armed themselves for a struggle to unite "their" respective population centers in Bosnia with their "homelands."

The Bosnian Serbs, under the aggressive national leadership of Radovan Karadžić (who was later in The Hague put on trial for, and convicted of, genocide, among other crimes), set up a Bosnian Serb Republic in January 1992. By the beginning of April, despite Izetbegović's initial hopes of inducing the Serbs and Croats to join in a new democratic Bosnia, open warfare between the rival ethnic groups had broken out in Bosnia. Especially at the outset, the Serbs had by far the better of the war. Poorly armed Bosnian Muslim police units were no match for the Serbs, who were equipped with Yugoslav Peoples' Army weapons and armored vehicles that were turned over to the infant Bosnian Serb Army.

The ethnic-cleansing campaigns carried out by the Bosnian Serb Army and their associated militias (backed by Belgrade) involved some 3,600 towns and villages in Bosnia-Herzegovina and hundreds of thousands of Bosnian Muslims.[4] The fundamental idea was to drive the Muslims—men, women, and children—from their homes in territory that the Serbs claimed as their own. The means of ethnic cleansing varied depending on the size and the location of the Muslim population. Sometimes outright military assaults, including tanks and artillery, would precede the cleansing of towns. But usually, the job of getting rid of the Muslim population was left to militias, some no more than armed gangs of right-wing, nationalist thugs, who would kill, maim, rape, and beat village residents, burn their homes, and send them packing, sometimes on foot, sometimes on buses that were arranged for the purpose. Local recruits, who operated in the vicinity of their own towns and villages, joined the Serb paramilitaries.[5] This made the violence up close and personal, as old scores were settled, new ones imagined, and neighbors attacked neighbors.[6] Serbs who tried to help their Bosnian friends were isolated and assaulted by co-nationals. The idea was to instill terror in the local Muslim population and induce them to run for their lives.

The genocidal treatment of the Muslim population in the first months of the war was concentrated in a series of makeshift detention facilities and prisons set up by the Bosnian Serbs for their victims. Ethnic cleansing is as much about punishment as it is about expulsion. This was nowhere clearer than in the terrifying Omarska prison camp, where some 6,000 people were incarcerated and endured the tortures of hell.[7] Between May and August of 1992, according to The Hague Tribunal, guards "regularly and openly killed, raped, tortured, beat and otherwise subject prisoners to conditions of constant humiliation, degradation and fear of death."[8] Željko Mejakić, the commander of the camp in Omarska, was the first person indicted by the Tribunal for genocide.[9] At Keraterm, a camp outside of Prijedor, Serb guards and overseers seemed to derive pleasure from regularly beating and bloodying their prisoners with every instrument imaginable: "wooden batons, metal rods, baseball bats, lengths of thick industrial cable that had metal balls affixed at their end, rifle butts, and knives."[10] The beatings routinely resulted in the death of their victims.

The ethnic cleansing included rape, often on the spot, sometimes in transit, and sometimes in specially designed rape camps, as a way to torment the Bosnian Muslims. The Helsinki report on Bosnia, which relied on interviews with many rape victims, stated:

> Soldiers attacking villages have raped women and girls in their homes, in front of family members and in the village square. Women have

been arrested and raped during interrogation. In some villages and towns, women and girls have been gathered together and taken to holding centers—often schools or community sports halls—where they are raped, gang-raped and abused repeatedly sometimes for days or even weeks at a time. Other women have been taken seemingly at random from their communities or out of a group of refugees with which they are traveling and raped by soldiers.

The report continued that the women they interviewed emphasized "how they were gang raped, taunted with ethnic slurs and cursed by rapists who stated their intention forcibly to impregnate women as a haunting reminder of the rape and an intensification of the trauma it inflicts."[11] Some Serb perpetrators thought of rape as a way to destroy Muslim identity and restore the good "Serb blood" that had been tainted by the long Ottoman occupation. Sometimes the violent pornographic fantasies of the soccer hoodlums, who were easily recruited by the paramilitary gangs, were unleashed while they held power over Bosnian women and girls.[12]

The attacks on the Bosnian Muslims were also murderous. The artillery bombardment from the hills surrounding Sarajevo cost many Muslims their lives. The Bosnian Serb campaigns of ethnic cleansing included periodic killing and executions. Approximately 100,000 people lost their lives and 2.2 million people were displaced in the fighting and campaigns of ethnic cleansing in Bosnia, by far the largest number of them Muslims. But until July 1995, when General Ratko Mladić and the Bosnian Serb army took control of Srebrenica, it would have been difficult to talk about "genocide" in Bosnia, since the Serb campaigns against Muslim civilians, as brutal and reprehensible as they were, did not include the kind of purposeful, planned mass killing actions that one knows from other cases of genocide.

The situation changed markedly at Srebrenica. The U.N. had designated the region a "safe area" in April 1993, meaning its civilian population was ostensibly protected by the presence of a contingent of U.N. troops—in this case, from the Netherlands, the "Dutchbat" or Dutch Battalion, of 570 lightly armed soldiers under the flag of UNPROFOR, the U.N. Protection Force. The inability of U.N. troops to stand up to the Bosnian Serb military, given the general lack of air support or serious reinforcements, was manifest. In fact, the Dutch showed remarkable indifference and lack of courage in the face of the initial incursions of the Drina Corps of the Bosnian Serb army on July 2, 1995.[13]

The population of the town of Srebrenica itself was swollen with Muslim refugees from the countryside, as the Serbs marched unimpeded into the "safe area." Other Muslims left in treks of refugees over the mountains in the direction of Žepa. Most Srebrenica Muslims headed northward to the Dutchbat headquarters in a huge battery factory in Potočari. Despite the efforts of the Dutch soldiers to keep them out, the refugees—several thousand women and men, young and old—managed to find ways to sneak through the fences and crowded into the grounds and buildings, hoping to find protection from the Bosnian Serb forces. Close to 20,000 hungry and miserable refugees gathered around the perimeter of the factory grounds, also hoping to be rescued by the U.N. troops.

The Bosnian Serb Drina Corps quickly made its way to Potočari. A journalist described the scene on the morning of July 12:

> Serb soldiers began arriving in the field at about noon, just five or six at first, then dozens more. They were mostly clean-shaven men, middle-aged or younger. They wore army and police uniforms. Dutch troops formed a cordon around the Muslims, but after Serb soldiers threatened to use force, the gates to the UN base were opened and the Dutch troops allowed the Serbs to take their weapons and roam freely.... Women cried. Soldiers drunk on plum brandy belched out songs with crude lyrics. They fired bullets into the air and began leading the menfolk away.[14]

For those outside the compound, this meant beating, rape, and mayhem. The Serb soldiers seized the Muslim men and packed off Muslim women and children on buses and trucks toward Muslim-ruled Bosnia. Getting on board a bus did not mean safe passage. Periodically, Bosnian Serb militiamen and paramilitaries stopped the buses, brutally harassed the women and girls while looking for money and jewelry, and sometimes removed the older boys and a few women and took them away. A high court in the Netherlands ruled in September 2013 that the Dutch battalion and the Dutch government were legally responsible for having turned over the Muslim refugees to the Serbs and were liable for their deaths.[15]

The commander of the Bosnian Serb Army, General Ratko Mladić, arrived later that day, as the job of sending away the Muslims was almost completed. The men and older boys were taunted and humiliated, sometimes beaten and tortured, before being taken to detention centers for so-called verification. Either they were shot or had their throats cut, or they were trucked off to other locations where they would eventually be executed and buried in mass graves. As described by an eyewitness to the Srebrenica massacre, Dražen Erdemović, busloads of men, blindfolded with their arms tied behind their backs, were transported

The exhumation of a mass grave in Potočari in 2007. The process of identifying victims in mass graves in Bosnia was extremely difficult because Bosnian Serb forces frequently dug up and reburied the victims in mass graves in scattered locations. The use of DNA technology has assisted specialists in reassembling victims' bodies. Photo by Adam Jones, Global Photo Archive/Flickr

to killing fields scattered around Potočari. There they were executed by firing squads and buried in mass graves. Erdemović described the process: "Another bus arrived. Each one held approximately sixty men. As the morning passed, the execution squad kept having to move to new positions. Rows of dead bodies were slowly filling up the field." They buried the corpses with bulldozers. Estimates of the total number killed at Srebrenica range between seven and eight thousand.[16]

A month later in the Security Council, the U.S. ambassador to the United Nations, Madeline Albright, denounced the killings and called for U.N. intervention, while waving photographs of the mass graves taken by U.S. intelligence satellites. In fact, Srebrenica served as a turning point in the West's readiness to intervene in the conflict, after years of hesitation. Eventually, the ICTY and the ICC ruled that the massacre in Srebrenica should be considered genocide, as the Bosnian Serbs had attempted to eliminate the Bosnian Muslim population of Srebrenica by driving off and killing a substantial part.[17] With the military hierarchy of the Bosnian Serbs directly implicated in the chain of events that led to genocide, and Slobodan Milošević and Radovan Karadžić apparently in the know about the murders, the courts concluded that Srebrenica constituted the purposeful killing of a designated group of Bosnian Muslims, thus genocide, and not a random massacre.

At the same time that ethnic cleansing and genocide erupted in the Balkans, Rwanda, located in the Great Lakes region of sub-Saharan Africa, experienced some of the most intense killing of the twentieth century. The Great Lakes area is the home of the Hutu and Tutsi peoples, who make up the largest part of the population and dominate the political systems of Rwanda and Burundi. According to the "Hamitic Theory" that the German and Belgian colonial authorities propagated, the primarily cattle-raising Tutsi came originally from the north and were tall, supple, intelligent, and racially superior to the farmer Hutu people, who were seen as short, stocky, "Negroid," and backward. Not surprisingly given these stereotypes, the colonial administrations and the native kings upon whom they relied favored the Tutsi aristocracy, which fared much better socially and economically than their Hutu counterparts. The Belgians issued identity cards to Tutsi and Hutu, undermining the relatively fluid inter-communal contacts between them, including intermarriage and economic commingling.[18]

Certainly before colonialism, the distinctions between Hutu and Tutsi were based more on lineage than ethnic origin. Marriage or increasing wealth could change one's designation. Despite the fact that the Tutsi and Hutu shared many common traits, including language and religious beliefs, the differences between them were reified by the experience of the colonial system of indirect rule through the local Tutsi elites.

The fratricidal killing between Hutu and Tutsi that has characterized so much of the history of the Great Lakes region since independence in the early 1960s needs to be thought of as a single narrative with a number of complex and intersecting stories. There is no single beginning and, unfortunately, no conclusive ending. In the oral traditions of both peoples, stories of past ill-treatment and massacres at the hand of the other were passed on in song and poetry, whether in the same locations or far away as exiles in one or the other of the lands of the Great Lakes region.[19]

During most of the forty-year history of Rwanda before 1994, ethnic peace had been more prevalent than strife.[20] But the majority-ruling Hutu in Rwanda were well aware of the dangers that a Tutsi-dominated military could pose to the Hutu population, given the post-colonial history of Tutsi belligerence against Hutu in Burundi.[21] To add to those

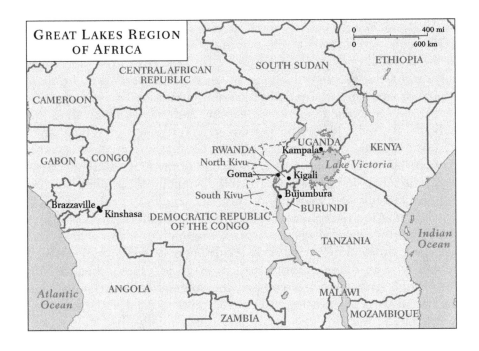

GREAT LAKES REGION OF AFRICA

fears, as many as 300,000 frightened Hutu refugees fled into Rwanda from Burundi during attacks by the Tutsi army in 1993 that followed several Hutu uprisings.[22]

To add to the regional turmoil, Rwandan Tutsi refugees in Uganda had formed the Rwandan Patriotic Front (RPF), whose military branch made repeated incursions into Rwanda in the period of civil war, 1990–1993. The Hutus were afraid that the Tutsi—called *inyenzi* (cockroaches) because of their night attacks across the border, and snakes because of their ostensibly treacherous actions—were intent on seizing power in Rwanda and taking back the land that had been given to Hutus. The attacks by the RPF served as a convenient pretext for the Hutus to arrest, persecute, and sometimes kill domestic Tutsi.

The Arusha Accords of August 1993 established a ceasefire between the RPF, which occupied the northern corner of Rwanda, and the Hutu government in the capital, Kigali. It also called for a transitional phase of Hutu-Tutsi power sharing until an election could be held. Finally, it created a U.N. force (UNAMIR), which was commanded by the Canadian General Roméo Dallaire, to be deployed to the country. These events mobilized the Hutu extremists critical of the long-time President Juvénal Habyarimana, a moderate Hutu, to demand that their privileges be protected against potential Tutsi advances. At the same time, the radical youth wing of the president's party formed militia groups in the early 1990s, trained by the Rwandan army and police. These were called the *interahamwe* ("those who attack together") and ended up playing a crucial role in the genocide. Some of these militia groups collected names of Tutsi to be eliminated in the event of a conflict.[23] The growing nationalism of the "Hutu Power" movement and the anti-Tutsi propaganda of the important Hutu extremist radio station added to tensions in the country, despite the formal progress that had been made in Arusha.

General Dallaire was so worried about plans, leaked by an *interahamwe* informant, to kill Belgian soldiers and parliamentary deputies, along with the discovery of an arms cache, that on January 11, 1994, he faxed his superiors at the U.N., asking permission to confiscate the arms. They denied his request. Dallaire's informant also revealed that the *interahamwe* militia had been trained to kill up to 1,000 Tutsis in twenty minutes.[24] Such was the state of the country when, on April 6, 1994, the plane carrying Rwandan President Habyarimana and Burundian President Ntaryamira back from peace talks in Dar es Salaam was shot down—it is unclear by whom—over Kigali airport.

Almost immediately after the announcement that Habyarimana had been killed, the Presidential Guard, presumably under the orders of the improvised Hutu Power interim authority led by Colonel Théoneste Bagosora, began the execution of important Tutsi politicians and of Hutu known to be sympathetic to a coalition government. Ministers from the coalition government were among the first to die, including the prime minister, the president of the supreme court, and almost all the leaders of the Social Democratic Party. Rwandan army soldiers, just as predicted by Dallaire's message, executed ten Belgian U.N. soldiers, prompting the withdrawal of Belgium's contingent in UNAMIR, effectively crippling the U.N.'s potential for containing the conflict.

Meanwhile, the fighting between the Rwandan Patriotic Front's troops (RPA) and the Rwandan army quickly resumed, with the RPA advances forcing the interim government to flee to Gitarama, where the killing of the Tutsi and moderate Hutu continued. Roadblocks were set up in the regions controlled by the interim government, manned by Rwandan army personnel and militia members. Tutsi were either killed on the spot or arrested and placed in detention. Lists of the Tutsi and moderate Hutu circulated within the militias, who hunted them down and murdered them. According to militant Hutu propaganda, Habyarimana was killed by the Tutsi; normal Hutu citizens would be next unless the Tutsi were eliminated first.

The massacre of Tutsi by Hutu militias and by civilians armed with machetes "spread like wildfire."[25] The militants now called on Hutu patriots to cut down their Tutsi enemies. On April 12, 1994, Radio Rwanda did not have to mention the Tutsi by name when it announced: "We need to unite against the enemy, the only enemy and this is the enemy that we have always known.... [I]t's the enemy who wants to reinstate the former feudal monarchy."[26] The killing of Tutsi men and women of all ages was vicious and thorough. One Hutu propagandist railed that the earlier killing of Tutsi mistakenly left Tutsi children alive; another extremist Hutu stated that the Tutsi would be eliminated completely so that "their children, later on, would not know what a Tutsi looked like, unless they referred to history books."[27]

In the patrilineal society of Rwanda, Tutsi wives of Hutu were sometimes spared, as were their children. The Hutu wives of Tutsi might be spared, but their children were routinely murdered. Hutu were beaten and harassed by their compatriots if they refused to participate in the killing. Those Hutu who tried to calm the perpetrators were also threatened. Noted one eyewitness: "They would call you an accomplice, and if you were called an accomplice you were killed like all the others."[28]

Tutsi peasants killed by the Rwandan army at Nyanza Hill in April 1994. The remains of more than 6,000 victims of the genocide are buried at the Nyanza Genocide Memorial Center. Altogether the Rwandan genocide claimed 800,000 victims. Photography by Patrick Robert/Sygma/CORBIS

Hutu who hid Tutsi friends or relations from the militia groups were also frequently killed, sometimes after being forced to kill their friends, neighbors, and relatives themselves. The perpetrators also looted while killing, apparently feeling the need to steal Tutsi property, slaughter and eat their animals, and burn down their houses, so that they would not return.

The rape and sexual slavery of Tutsi women and girls frequently accompanied the killing. Women were tortured and horribly abused before dying. Rape was so widespread and systematic that the ICTR included it in the genocide indictment, not just in the indictment for crimes against humanity, which formally includes rape, torture, forced deportation, and other similar transgressions. The prosecutors found evidence that the *interahamwe* paraded Tutsi women around naked to show off "the thighs of Tutsi women" and talked about finding out about "what a Tutsi woman tastes like," concluding:

> This sexualized representation of ethnic identity graphically illustrates that Tutsi women were subjected to sexual violence because they were Tutsi. Sexual violence was a step in the process of destruction of the Tutsi group—destruction of the spirit, of the will to live, and of life itself.[29]

Between April 6, when the president's plane crashed, and July 18, 1994, when the RPF ousted the interim government and took control of Rwanda, more than 800,000 people were killed, roughly 8,000 per day. Three-quarters of Rwanda's Tutsi population were eliminated. As many as 50,000 of those killed were Hutu.[30] If the RPF had not intervened, it is likely that no Tutsi would have escaped the clutches of the genocidal program of the Rwandan government.

On assuming power in Rwanda, the RPF, led by the Tutsi Paul Kagame, intensified a program of widespread retribution killings of Hutu. The Hutu were in any case so terrified of what the Tutsi would do to them that they fled in the millions to Tanzania, Uganda, and especially Zaire (since 1997 the Democratic Republic of the Congo, DRC). Approximately 1 million (some estimate up to 1.5 million) Hutu civilians, plus the more or less intact civilian government and army structure, fled to the west into eastern Zaire. Probably as many as a million Hutus fled to Tanzania to the east. Among the refugees to Zaire was the leadership of the *interahamwe*, including many of the most fervent organizers of the genocide in Rwanda. The refugee camps in North and South Kiva, the eastern provinces of Zaire, quickly turned into centers of Hutu governance and political ambitions. "The enemy had not been defeated," wrote an insightful journalist, "it had just run away."[31]

The horrors of Tutsi–Hutu fratricidal attacks have continued in eastern Congo until this very day, complicated by underdevelopment, the lure of mineral wealth, territorial ambitions of the Rwandan government, and the ineffectiveness of Congolese military and legal institutions.

Just as Tutsi and Hutu cannot be considered fixed ethnic categories, yet became markers for murder and genocide, the paradoxes of identity also permeated the killing in Darfur, the westernmost part of Sudan, in the early twenty-first century. The perpetrators were most often the so-called Janjaweed militias, who were of primarily Arab ethnicity. (Both the perpetrators and victims were Muslim.) *Janjaweed* means "armed men [devils] on horseback," and indicated that these militia groups operated for the most part on horses or camels. They called their victims "blacks" or "slaves," which related to the fact that, for the most part, the Janjaweed attacked three tribes with black African origins: the Fur, the Zaghawa, and the Masalit. There were people of mixed ethnicity among these tribes; most salient differences between them were not necessarily ethnic but, rather, social and economic ones.

The black African groups in Darfur were primarily tied to the life of village agriculture, while the Janjaweed mostly originated in groups of Arab pastoralist nomads, who came into conflict with the villagers over water, land, and other resources, as the lands of Darfur, as elsewhere in North Africa, turned increasingly into desert. As in Rwanda, the Darfur conflict saw ethnic categories hardened through the struggle itself, which emerged initially in 2002 and 2003 with the formation of rebel groups among the black African tribes. Their goal was to distribute Sudan's resources more equitably between Khartoum, the capital (and its immediate vicinity), and the rest of the immense country, the largest in Africa before the independence of South Sudan, in 2011.

Violence between Arab pastoralists and black African farmers escalated in the course of the 1990s, as a series of droughts and food shortages sharpened conflicts over water and land. As a result, the insurgents attacked Sudanese military and police installations in the spring of 2003. The response on the part of the Sudanese government, led by its President Omar al-Bashir, was extreme: all-out war against the black African tribes of Darfur. "Our priority from now on," stated al-Bashir in December 2003, "is to eliminate the rebellion, and any outlaw element is our target.... We will use the army, the police, the mujahedeen, the horsemen to get rid of the rebellion."[32] From Khartoum's point of view, the rebellious tribes started the fighting in Darfur, which was met by appropriate counterinsurgency measures.

Sudanese President Omar Hassan al-Bashir addresses Sudan's Parliament in Khartoum on April 1, 2013. Al-Bashir was indicted for genocide in Darfur by the International Criminal Court in 2010, but he has repeatedly avoided arrest, despite traveling to other countries under treaty obligations to arrest and turn him over to The Hague. Charges of crimes against humanity have also been leveled at al-Bashir as a result of bombing campaigns in the Nuba region of South Sudan. Photo by Abd Raouf/AP

The "mujahedeen, the horsemen" to whom al-Bashir referred were the Janjaweed militias, who were armed and paid by the Sudanese government to engage in attacks against the rebels, with the intention of clearing out black African towns and villages and crushing their inhabitants' will to resist. The Janjaweed were promised land from the holdings of their victims, which explains some of the thoroughness of the ethnic cleansing involved.[33] These attacks grew particularly intense in the fall of 2003 and the beginning of 2004. The Sudanese army, along with air support, including helicopter gunships, sometimes inaugurated the conflict by assaulting supposed centers of rebel support. The attacks usually came early in the morning, before people awoke, and were accompanied by militia raids, which wreaked havoc on the villages, burning homes, raping women, and randomly shooting the inhabitants.

The scenes were horrific, as the Janjaweed appeared to have been given full quarter by their government sponsors to loot and rape at will. A very large number of young girls and women were abducted and subject to gang rape and serial rape. This seemed a particularly vicious way that the "superior" Arab Janjaweed could insult and demean the allegedly inferior black Africans. Many women and girls ended up pregnant; some were told that they would have superior Arab babies as a result. One victim stated: "They kill our males and dilute our blood with rape. [They] want to finish us as a people, end our history."[34] The infrastructures of the villages were destroyed; farm implements and crops were leveled, irrigation pumps blown up, and wells poisoned so that no one would return. Sometimes the Janjaweed themselves came back to sites of the attacks to make sure no survivors returned or stragglers remained, a common tactic of genocidaires. More than seven hundred villages were completely or partly destroyed.[35]

The U.S. Department of State, in its efforts to determine whether the violence in Darfur should have been designated genocide, interviewed some 1,136 randomly chosen refugees in Chad from a group of approximately 200,000. The results demonstrate the extent of violence that the refugees endured during the Janjaweed attacks. Sixty-one percent of the interviewees had experienced the killing of a family member; 16 percent had seen or experienced rape (often more than once); 81 percent had seen their villages destroyed.[36] One interview report from the Gaga Refugee Camp in eastern Chad describes the attacks:

> The government [of Sudan] used planes and trucks to attack us and the *Janjaweed* came on horse and camels and on foot. They came in the early morning just before sunrise and I was asleep. I first knew there was an attack because I heard the sound of weapons from the planes and trucks. As soon as I heard the sounds I got up and ran from the hut. As we ran I heard some *Janjaweed* scream "*Nuba afnine*" ["Nuba shit"]. I don't know how many *Janjaweed* and soldiers there were but maybe it was around 200. So many I can't count. Maybe 20 green and black [camouflaged] Landcruisers and hundreds of horses and camels.
>
> The soldiers and *Janjaweed* chased us and they kept shooting men and boys. Many were killed. They also caught men and slashed them with long knives on the legs and arms, cutting off their arms and legs.... Some who had their legs cut off were able to move, some could not.[37]

The problem for many from the Fur, Masalit, and Zaghawa tribes was that they were driven from their lands into towns or holding camps in Darfur that were at the mercy of Janjaweed and government soldiers. Nearly 1.65 million inhabitants (out of a population of 6 million) were internally displaced within Darfur. The U.N. Commission described the fate of the people of Kailek, a predominantly Fur village in the south of Darfur. The village had served as a gathering point for villagers from the surrounding area who had already been driven from their homes. The Janjaweed returned, driving out the inhabitants and "hunting down the villagers" as they fled to the mountains. According to the U.N., "People were shot when, suffering from thirst, they were forced to leave their hiding places to go to water points." Those who surrendered were "summarily shot and killed." Those who returned to Kailek or were seized, about 30,000 people altogether, were confined in a small area. Many were tortured and executed.

"Men who were in confinement in Kailek were called out and shot in front of everyone." "There are reports of people being thrown onto fires to burn to death. There are reports that people were partially skinned or otherwise injured and left to die."[38]

Much as in Bosnia and Rwanda, rape was a terrifying and ubiquitous threat to the displaced black African women in Darfur. In Tawila, in southern Darfur, a girls' boarding school was attacked in February 2004. The Janjaweed forced their way into the school, "pointed their guns at the girls and forced them to strip naked," stealing their goods and valuables. Meanwhile, the girls—some 110 in all—were raped and abused.[39] Elsewhere, the Janjaweed abducted women and girls for several days, sometimes weeks on end, to be sexually assaulted in Janjaweed camps. At Wadi Tina in northern Darfur, one woman described being raped repeatedly:

> Over a period of a week, I was raped 14 times by different Janjaweed. I told them to stop. They said "you are women of Tora Bora and we will not stop this." We were called slaves and frequently beaten with leather straps, punched and slapped. I feared for my life if I do not have sex with them.[40]

Sometimes, the Janjaweed even branded the girls they raped as a way to ensure that they would be ostracized and demeaned.[41]

Repeated peace negotiations to bring the conflict in Darfur to an end have been frustrated from the beginning by the lack of interest by the Khartoum government and by the difficulty of achieving a united stance on the part of the rebel groups, which frequently are at odds with each other about their demands from the government. Although the level of violence in Darfur is much diminished from its height in 2003–2004, the region is by no means safe for black Africans, many hundreds of thousands of whom remain in refugee camps in Chad and Darfur with insufficient food and threatening conditions for survival.

Meanwhile, Khartoum has opened up another front in its counterinsurgency cum genocidal attacks on black Africans, and that is in the Nuba Mountains on the border with the newly created country of South Sudan. There, rebel groups under the banner of the Sudan People's Liberation Army fought for years to gain control of their own resources and political structure. The Sudanese army had already conducted a genocidal campaign against the Nuba peoples in the mid-1990s.[42] Left behind in the peace talks that created South Sudan, they have been intermittently bombed and strafed by the Sudanese Air Force. The result has been more violence, more hunger and disease, more deaths, and more displacement of peoples.

It is very difficult to know how many people were "killed" during the conflict in Darfur. So many died of privation and disease—from the harsh conditions as internal refugees or refugees in Chad—that the numbers are hard to assess. A variety of sources agree that somewhere in the neighborhood of 300,000 to 400,000 people lost their lives due to the Sudanese army and Janjaweed attacks in the period from 2003 to 2010.[43] Of those, some 80 percent died of disease, malnutrition, and exposure.[44]

When the depredations in Darfur first came to the attention of the international community, the U.S. administration of George W. Bush, led by his secretary of state, Colin Powell, came to the conclusion in September 2004 that the killing in Darfur was genocide and that the Sudanese government led by General Omar al-Bashir was responsible.[45] The U.N. was ready to condemn al-Bashir's policies as constituting war crimes and crimes against humanity, but explicitly rejected the claim that Khartoum's actions in Darfur should be considered genocide.[46] The International Criminal Court indicted al-Bashir for war crimes and crimes against humanity in March 2009 and issued a warrant for his arrest. But the prosecutors later came to the conclusion that he was also guilty of genocide and convinced the court to issue a second warrant for genocide in July 2010. There is much that we still do not know about al-Bashir's motives and the chain of command from Khartoum to the Janjaweed murderers. The ICC's indictment of genocide has a great deal of documentary support. But al-Bashir has refused to submit himself and other indicted Sudanese to the jurisdiction of the court, and so far he has not been arrested when he has traveled abroad.

The killing and rape have stopped in Bosnia. The creation of a separate Serb Republic within the Federation of Bosnia-Herzegovina, the result of the 1995 Dayton Agreement, has caused myriad problems for effectively governing Bosnia. Equally daunting for the unity of Bosnia are the unhealed wounds of ethnic cleansing, genocide, and mass rape suffered by the victims. The perpetrators, in this case the Bosnian Serbs, for the greatest part deny genocide and insist that they were as much victims as the Bosnian Muslims. That makes any kind of forgiveness or reconciliation all the harder for the Bosnian Muslims, who mourn their lost men and boys at Srebrenica and continue to identify bodies that were dispersed in mass graves throughout the region.

The memory of Tutsi military attacks on Hutu in Burundi was a powerful motivating factor for the creation of the "Hutu Power" movement in Rwanda, which then turned with extraordinary fury on the Tutsi, killing hundreds of thousands within several months. The Tutsi leadership of Rwanda used the images of that genocide to justify their own incursions into the Democratic Republic of Congo, based on the idea that they were only protecting their people from being slaughtered again by the Hutus and their allies. The effects of this long-term, ethnically charged killing, rape, displacement, and banditry are incalculable.

The violence in Darfur continues on a lower level than in 2003–2004. But the repercussions of that violence continue to have an important impact on the lives of the population. While some Darfur victims have returned "home" from refugee camps, for the most part their villages were destroyed and their lands ruined. Intermittent efforts at reconciliation between the Sudanese government and the black African population are spoiled by ongoing attacks by some rebel parties on government installations and episodic retaliation on the part of the government and its Janjaweed allies. The cases of Bosnia, Rwanda, and Darfur cease to capture the headlines. But the reverberations of genocide are profound.

Conclusion

Genocide was present—even ubiquitous—in many of the foundational documents of world civilization. The Old Testament, Homer's *Iliad*, and Thucydides. *History of the Peloponnesian Wars* describe the perpetration of genocide, even if the actual historical documentation of such events themselves is weak and inconclusive. In the ancient world, the bloodletting involved in setting apart and attacking groups of "others," whether for political, religious, or social reasons, was even more pervasive than in more modern times. One of the fundamental propositions underlying this short study is that late twentieth-century definitions of genocide unjustifiably privilege the "modern" and discount the longue durée when thinking about the problems of mass killing. This was notably *not* the case of Raphael Lemkin, who coined the term "genocide," provided it with a substantive definition, and engaged in the first world historical studies of the phenomenon.

The Spanish conquest of the Americas should be considered a genocidal event of world historical importance. As in the genocides of the ancient world, its victims were often enslaved and died from overwork and disease. The Spanish introduced a new racial element into their thinking about the native peoples. The Indians were inferior beings, not really human, and therefore justifiably deprived of their freedom and their lives. Two centuries earlier, racial considerations played no role in the Mongol domination of Eurasia. Mongol genocides were driven instead by the murderous imperatives of unchallenged rule: submit as a people or be eliminated, as many groups were.

The expansion of European empires introduced another crucial element into the history of genocide, and that was the conflict between the pastoral economies of settlers, who accompanied or followed the trail of empire, and the subsistence economies of the native peoples, who lived themselves in hunter-gatherer or pastoral communities. The question of who had the right to the land was emphatically decided by force in favor of the settlers, and, as a consequence, North American Indians,

Aborigines in the Antipodes, and native African tribes, among others, found themselves subjected to genocidal attacks and fighting for their very survival.

Colonial methods of genocide—concentration camps, forced deportation, land seizure, starvation, and racist categorizations—found their ways back to the European continent during the First World War. The genocide of the Herero and Nama by the Germans in South West Africa presaged in many ways the mass killing to come on the European continent during the First and Second World Wars. The Ottoman government's attack on its Armenian population in 1915, having recently marked its centennial, should be considered first and foremost against the backdrop of the history of the decline of the Ottoman Empire, the ascendance of the Young Turks, and the existential threats embodied in World War I.

Hitler's assault against the Jews, Sinti and Roma, Soviet POWs, and others derived primarily from internal German circumstances, going back especially to World War I and its enormous impact—psychological, emotional, territorial, economic, and financial—on the German people. Of course, German anti-Semitism, both traditional and in its virulent Nazi iteration, also played a profound role. As we know, Hitler was aware of the Armenian genocide and the lack of international reaction to its perpetration. He understood that international society would not stand in the way of his murderous plans.

With a somewhat broader definition of genocide than used by the 1948 U.N. Convention, one that includes the intentional elimination of social and political groups, communist and anti-communist mass killing can and should be included in a narrative history of genocide. In terms of sheer numbers, the communist genocides of Stalin and Mao are unequaled events in the twentieth century. Pol Pot's killing of Cambodian citizens was unrivaled in proportional terms. But communist genocides, which derived in good part from the unattainable Utopian visions of powerful Marxist-Leninist dictators, were frequently matched in their intensity and murderousness by anti-communist genocides. The Cold War and the assumed "inevitable" struggle between communist and capitalist countries set a nurturing environment for both communist and anti-communist genocides.

The conclusion of the Cold War did not bring an end to the history of genocide, any more than it ensured the unchallenged ascendance of liberal and capitalist ideas of organizing societies. The wars in the Balkans in the 1990s and the conflict over the fate of Yugoslavia produced genocide, ethnic cleansing, and the destruction of multinational societies. The tragedy in Bosnia alerted the international community to the dangers of ethnic conflict, but also to the potential of interdiction and intervention. Despite the determination of the U.N. to introduce the "Responsibility to Protect" into the behavior of nations, Darfur, in particular, was a shocking example of twenty-first-century genocide that was impervious to worldwide condemnation.

Even if the international community now finds itself constrained by a variety of circumstances to act concertedly in Syria to prevent mass killing, the Assad regime will be held accountable for its depredations by the International Criminal Court, which began its work on July 1, 2002, to deal judicially with precisely such actions. If the news from Syria is worrisome, the situation in eastern Congo and the Great Lakes region seems to have settled down as a consequence of coordinated U.N. and African Union involvement.

There are many similarities in the cases of genocide over the past three millennia. War, above all, serves as the seedbed for genocide. The activity of military confrontation and destruction frequently "bleeds" into genocide. The dehumanization of alleged enemies, external in the case of war or potential war, or internal in the case of the struggle to assert political supremacy, predates and accompanies genocidal campaigns. The rape of women, which includes the forcible abduction of females into the perpetrators' families as slaves and wives, also figures into many cases of genocide over its history. The attempt of empires to spread their territories and consolidate their gains through colonization and settlement involves the removal of indigenous peoples, which too frequently culminates in genocide. The admixture of imperialism and racism has proven particularly lethal over time for those peoples who originally lived in territories subjected to colonial rule. It also has had a combustible half-life in the post-colonial period, influencing outbreaks of genocidal violence even after independence. Religion and ideology, like race thinking, often have framed campaigns of genocide, providing convenient stereotypes of the victims and justifications for the perpetrators. Have changing international norms induced us to find ways to limit the perspectives of genocide by identifying and combatting its components? Have our "better angels" made it possible to speak of the end of the world history of genocide?[1] Probably not. But understanding its history can only help us get there.

Chronology

1020–930 BCE
Beginning of the Kingdom of Israel
(approx.)

800 BCE
Rise of the Greek city-states

431–404 BCE
Peloponnesian War

149–146 BCE
Third Punic War between Rome and
Carthage

1095
Pope Urban calls for First Crusade

1206
Establishment of Mongol empire under
Genghis Khan

1208
Pope Innocent III calls for Albigensian
Crusade against Cathars

1492
Christopher Columbus reaches the New
World

1519–1521
Hernán Cortés leads the Spanish
Conquest of Mexico

1524–1530
Francisco Pizarro's campaigns against
the Incas

1824–1832
"Black War" with Aborigines in Van
Diemen's Land (Tasmania)

1856–1864
Elimination of the Yuki in Round Valley
(Mendocino County, California)

1904–1907
Herero Wars in German South West
Africa

April 24, 1915
Armenian Genocide Day; first victims
arrested in Istanbul

1932–1933
Ukrainian hunger famine (Holodomor)

September 1, 1939
Nazi invasion of Poland; killing of Jews
and Poles begins

January 20, 1942
Wannsee Conference plans "Final
Solution" of the "Jewish Question"

January 1958
Mao launches the Great Leap Forward

September 30, 1965
Coup attempt in Indonesia; sets off
massacres of communists

April 12, 1975
Phnom Penh falls to Khmer Rouge;
Cambodian genocide begins

December 7, 1975
Indonesian military invade East Timor

April 6, 1994
Downing of airplane carrying Rwandan
President Habyarimana; beginning of the
Rwandan genocide

July 1995
Genocide at Srebrenica

2003–2010
Crisis in Darfur

2009–2010
President Omar al-Bashir indicted by
International Criminal Court for war
crimes, crimes against humanity, and
genocide

Notes

INTRODUCTION

1. Rome Statute of the International Criminal Court (as corrected by the procès-verbaux of November 10, 1998, and July 12, 1999).
2. John Cooper, *Raphael Lemkin and the Struggle for the Genocide Convention* (New York: Palgrave Macmillan, 2008); Samantha Power, *"A Problem from Hell": America and the Age of Genocide* (New York: Basic Books, 2002); Norman M. Naimark, *Stalin's Genocides* (Princeton, NJ: Princeton University Press, 2010), 15–29.
3. Cited in Power, *"A Problem from Hell,"* 521n6.
4. Raphael Lemkin, *Axis Rule in Occupied Europe: Laws of Occupation, Analysis of Government Proposals for Redress* (Washington, DC: Carnegie Endowment for International Peace, 1944), 79.
5. Nehemiah Robinson, *The Genocide Convention: A Commentary* (New York: Institute of Jewish Affairs, 1960), 17–18; see Resolution 96(I) in appendix 1, 121–22; my emphasis.
6. "The Convention on the Prevention and Punishment of the Crime of Genocide," in *Totally Unofficial: Raphael Lemkin and the Genocide Convention*, ed. Adam Strom et al. (Brookline, MA: Facing History and Ourselves, 2007), 38.
7. William A. Schabas, *Genocide in International Law,* 2nd ed. (Cambridge: Cambridge University Press, 2009), 95–116.
8. See David Scheffer, *All the Missing Souls: A Personal History of the War Crimes Tribunals* (Princeton, NJ: Princeton University Press, 2012).
9. See Ben Kiernan, *Blood and Soil: A World History of Genocide and Extermination from Sparta to Darfur* (New Haven: Yale University Press, 2007), 43–71.
10. Hannah Arendt, *The Origins of Totalitarianism* (San Diego: Harcourt Brace, 1979), 123. See the work of Jürgen Zimmerer, including, "War Concentration Camps and Genocide: The First German Genocide," in *Genocide in German Southwest Africa: The Colonial War (1904–1908) in Namibia and its Aftermath*, ed. Jürgen Zimmerer and Joachim Zellar (Monnwirth: Merlin Press, 2008), 47–59.
11. Eric Weitz, *A Century of Genocide: Utopias of Race and Nation* (Princeton, NJ: Princeton University Press, 2003), 46.
12. Isabel Hull, "Military Culture and the Production of 'Final Solutions' in the Colonies," in *The Specter of Genocide: Mass Murder in Historical Perspective*, ed. Robert Gellately and Ben Kiernan (Cambridge: Cambridge University Press, 2003), 141–44.
13. See Norman M. Naimark, *Fires of Hatred: Ethnic Cleansing in 20th Century Europe* (Cambridge, MA: Harvard University Press, 2001), 57.

CHAPTER 1

1. Exodus 17:9:16, 17:9:14. In this and further references, I use the King James version (KJV) of the Bible.
2. 1 Samuel 15:3.

3. 1 Samuel 15:8, 1 Samuel 15:33.

4. 1 Samuel 15:30:17.

5. Deuteronomy 7:22, 7:25

6. Exodus 23:33.

7. Deuteronomy 7:2.

8. Deuteronomy 7:5.

9. Douglas S. Earl, *The Joshua Delusion? Rethinking Genocide in the Bible* (Eugene, OR: Cascade Books, 2010), 53–54.

10. Deuteronomy 20:16.

11. Deuteronomy 20:18.

12. Joshua 6:21.

13. Joshua 6:26.

14. See Philip R. Davies' introduction to Thomas L. Thompson, *Biblical Narrative and Palestine's History: Changing Perspectives 2* (Sheffield: Equinox, 2013).

15. Israel Finkelstein and Neil Asher Silberman, *The Bible Unearthed: Archaeology's New Vision of Ancient Israel and the Origin of Its Sacred Texts* (New York: Simon and Schuster, 2002), 5.

16. Thompson, *Biblical Narrative and Palestine's History*, 154,

17. E. V. Rieu, trans., *The Iliad of Homer* (Baltimore: Penguin, 1950), 118.

18. Cited in Ben Kiernan, *Blood and Soil: A World History of Genocide and Extermination from Sparta to Darfur* (New Haven: Yale University Press, 2007), 60.

19. Thucydides, *History of the Peloponnesian War*, 5.17.

20. Ibid., 2.7. Cited in Kiernan, *Blood and Soil*, 48.

21. Fernand Braudel, *Memory and the Mediterranean* (New York: Vintage Books, 2002), 281.

22. Mary T. Boatwright, Daniel J. Gargola, and Richard J. A. Talbert, *A Brief History of the Romans* (Oxford: Oxford University Press, 2006), 77.

CHAPTER 2

1. Cited in Morris Rossabi, *The Mongols and Global History* (New York: Norton, 2011), 1.

2. Steven Pinker, *The Better Angels of Our Nature: Why Violence Has Declined* (New York: Penguin, 2011), 190–99.

3. R. J. Rummel, *Death by Government* (New Brunswick, NJ: Transaction, 2004), 51.

4. Yaqut al-Hamawi, cited in Ian Morris, *Why the West Rules—For Now: The Patterns of History and What They Reveal About the Future* (New York: Farrar, Straus and Giroux, 2010), 389.

5. 'Alā' al-Dīn 'Aṭā Malik Juvaynī, from text of Mirza Muhammad Qazvini, *The History of the World Conquerer*, trans. by John Andrew Boyle, vol. I (Cambridge, MA: Harvard University Press, 1958), 123–29.

6. J. J. Saunders, *The History of the Mongol Conquests* (London: Routledge and Kegan Paul, 1971), reprinted in Frank Chalk and Kurt Johansson, *The History and Sociology of Genocide: Analyses and Case Studies* (New Haven: Yale University Press, 1990), 105.

7. Ibid., 106.

8. Morris, *Why the West Rules*, 391.

9. Janos M. Bak and Martyn Rady, eds., trans., annots., *Master Roger's Epistle to the Sorrowful Lament upon the Destruction of the Kingdom of Hungary by the Tatars*, (Budapest: CEU Press, 2010), 169–171.

10. Ibid., 185, 187, 189.

11. Ibid., 199.

12. Ibid., 201.

13. Ibid., 205, 207.

14. Ibid., 217.

15. See Ian Morris, *Why the West Rules*, 392.

16. Bak and Rady, *Master Roger's Epistle*, 205.

17. Fulcher of Chartres, in August C. Krey, *The First Crusade: The Accounts of Eye-Witnesses and Participants* (Princeton, NJ: Princeton University Press, 1921), 29.

18. In Krey, *The First Crusade*; see Robert the Monk, 30, and Bolderic of Dol, 35.

19. Eudes of Châteauroux, Sermon I, in Christoph T. Maier, *Crusade Propaganda and Ideology: Model Sermons for the Preaching of the Cross* (Cambridge: Cambridge University Press, 2000), 141.

20. See Norman Housely, "Crusades Against Christians: Their Origins and Early Development, c. 1000–1216," in *The Crusades: The Essential Readings*, ed. Thomas F. Madden (Oxford: Blackwell, 2002), 71–72.

21. Raymond D'Aguilers, *Historia Francorum Qui Ceperunt Iherusalem*, trans., with intro. and notes by John Hugh Hill and Laurita L. Hill (Philadelphia: American Philosophical Society, 1968), 40, 48.

22. Ibid., 73

23. Ibid., 81–84.

24. Ibid., 125.

25. Ibid., 128n22.

26. Cited in Thomas F. Madden, "Rivers of Blood: An Analysis of One Aspect of the Crusader Conquest of Jerusalem in 1099," *Revista chilena de Estudios Medievales* 1 (January-June 2012): 29.

27. Housley, "Crusades Against Christians," 85–88.

28. Ibid., 91.

29. Malise Ruthven, *Torture: The Grand Conspiracy* (London: Weidenfeld and Nicholson, 1978), in Frank Chalk and Kurt Johansson, *The History and Sociology of Genocide: Analyses and Case Studies* (New Haven: Yale University Press, 1990), 126.

30. Ibid., 126.

31. Cited in Joseph R. Strayer, *The Albigensian Crusades*, in Chalk and Johansson, *The History and Sociology of Genocide*, 119.

32. *The Chronicle of William of Puylaurens, The Albigensian Crusade and Its Aftermath*, trans. by W. A. Sibly and M. D. Sibly (Woodbridge: Boydell Press, 2003), 128.

33. Ruthven, *Torture*, 126.

34. Cited in Housely, "Crusades against Christians," 91.

CHAPTER 3

1. J. M. Roberts, *The Penguin History of Europe* (London: Penguin, 1997), 234.

2. George M. Fredrickson, *Racism: A Short History* (Princeton, NJ: Princeton University Press, 2002), 31–42.

3. Tzvetan Todorov, *The Conquest of America: The Question of the Other* (Norman: University of Oklahoma Press, 1999), 133.

4. Jared Diamond, *Guns, Germs, and Steel: The Fates of Human Societies* (New York: W.W. Norton, 1999), 67, 78.

5. Bartolomé de Las Casas, *A Short Account of the Destruction of the Indies*, ed. and trans. by Nigel Griffen, with an introduction by Anthony Pagden (New York: Penguin, 1992), 24.

6. Todorov uses a variety of sources to describe these horrors in *The Conquest of America*, 134–43. For Motolinia's ten plagues that beset the Indians, see 137–38.

7. Juan Ginés de Sepúlveda, "On the Reasons for the Just War among the Indians (1547)," www.history.ubc.ca/sites/default/files/courses/documents/%5Brealname%5D/sepulveda_1547.pdf.

8. Ibid.

9. De Las Casas, *A Short Account*, 13.

10. See Mark Levene, *The Rise of the West and the Coming of Genocide*, vol. 2 (London: I. B. Taurus, 2005), 13.

11. Ben Kiernan, *Blood and Soil: A World History of Genocide and Extermination from Sparta to Darfur* (New Haven: Yale University Press, 2007), 80.

12. Todorov, *The Conquest of America*, 161–62.

13. De Las Casas, *A Short Account*, 13.

14. Cited in Todorov, *The Conquest of America*, 142.

15. Antonio de la Calancha (1638), in Ian Morris, *Why the West Rules—For Now: The Patterns of History and What They Reveal About the Future* (New York: Farrar, Straus and Giroux, 2010), 460.

16. John Cummins, *The Voyage of Christopher Columbus: Columbus's Own Journal of Discovery* (London: Weidenfeld, 1992), 97.

17. De Las Casas, *A Short Account*, 12.

18. Ibid., 29.

19. Ibid., 30.

20. Kiernan, *Blood and Soil*, 88.

21. Cited in Kiernan, *Blood and Soil*, 88.

22. Hernán Cortés, *Letters from Mexico*, trans. and ed. by A. R. Pagden (New York: Grossman, 1971), 59–62.

23. Kiernan, *Blood and Soil*, 89.

24. Cortés, *Letters*, 73.

25. Ibid.

26. Kiernan, *Blood and Soil*, 90.

27. Pagden, in Cortés, *Letters*, 465–66.

28. See Todorov, *The Conquest of America*, 55–62.

29. Kiernan, *Blood and Soil*, 91.

30. Cortés, *Letters*, 3. Todorov, *Conquest of America*, 60.

31. Kiernan, *Blood and Soil*, 88, 93.

32. De Las Casas, *A Short Account*, 68–74.

33. Jared Diamond replicates selections of those accounts in *Guns, Germs, and Steel*, 69–74. The section on the Incas is based on these.

34. Cited in Morris, *Why the West Rules*, 460.

35. Frank Chalk and Kurt Jonassohn, *The History and Sociology of Genocide: Analyses and Case Studies* (New Haven: Yale University Press, 1990), 178.

CHAPTER 4

1. Mark Levene places major emphasis on the role of the modern nation-state in the history of genocide, but dates its beginnings from the end of the seventeenth

century. Mark Levene, *Genocide in the Age of the Nation-State; vol. 1: The Meaning of Genocide* (London: I. B. Taurus, 2008), 15–22.

2. Nigel Penn, "The Destruction of Hunter-Gatherer Societies on the Pastoralist Frontier; The Cape and Australia Compared," in Mohamed Adhikari, *Genocide on Settler Frontiers: When Hunter Gatherers and Commercial Stock Farmers Clash* (Cape Town: Cape Town University Press, 2014), 159.

3. Lyndall Ryan, "'No Right to the Land': The Role of the Wool Industry in the Destruction of Aboriginal Societies in Tasmania (1817–1832) and Victoria (1835–1851)," in Adhikari, *Genocide on Settler Frontiers*, 189. Some estimates of the size of the aboriginal population are lower, 3,000 to 4,000.

4. Mark Levene, *The Rise of the West and the Coming of Genocide*, vol. 2 (London: I. B. Taurus, 2005), 38.

5. Lyndall Ryan, "'No Right to the Land,'" 188–89.

6. Levene, *The Rise of the West*, 38.

7. Henry Melville, *The History of Van Diemen's Land from the Year 1824 to 1835, Inclusive: During the Administration of Lieutenant-Governor George Arthur* (Sydney: Horwitz–Grahame, 1965), 30–31.

8. Ibid., 32–33. Emphasis in the original.

9. Levene, *The Rise of the West*, 40.

10. Ryan, "'No Right to the Land,'" 236.

11. Ibid.

12. James Morris, "The Final Solution, Down Under," *Horizon* 14, no. 1 (Winter 1972), reprinted in Frank Chalk and Kurt Jonassohn, *The History and Sociology of Genocide: Analyses and Case Studies* (New Haven: Yale University Press, 1990), 214.

13. Ann Curthoys, "Genocide in Tasmania: The History of an Idea," in *Empire, Colony, Genocide: Conquest, Occupation, and Subaltern Resistance in World History*, ed. A. Dirk Moses (New York: Berghahn, 2008), 230.

14. Ryan, "'No Right to the Land,'" 203–204.

15. See Benjamin Madley, "Reexamining the American Genocide Debate: Meaning, Historiography, and New Methods," *American Historical Review* 120 (1): 98–139.

16. Cited in Ben Kiernan, *Blood and Soil: A World History of Genocide and Extermination from Sparta to Darfur* (New Haven: Yale University Press, 2007), 231–34.

17. See Robert V. Remini, *Andrew Jackson and His Indian Wars* (New York: Viking, 2001), 169.

18. Lynwood Carranco and Estle Beard, *Genocide and Vendetta: The Round Valley Wars in Northern California* (Norman: University of Oklahoma Press, 1981), 126.

19. Benjamin Madley, "Patterns of Frontier Genocide 1803–1910: The Aboriginal Tasmanians, the Yuki of California, and the Herero of Namibia," *Journal of Genocide Research* 6, no. 2 (June 2004): 181.

20. *Majority and Minority Report of the Special Joint Committee on the Mendocino War*, Charles T. Botts, State Printer, 1860, 6.

21. Virginia P. Miller, *Ukomno'm: The Yuki Indians of Northern California* (Socorro, NM: Ballerina, 1979), 46. Carranco and Beard, *Genocide and Vendetta*, 14.

22. *Majority and Minority Report*, 49.

23. "Newspaper article, San Francisco, 1860," and "Indian Butcheries in California," in *The Destruction of the California Indians: A Collection of Documents from the Period 1847 to 1863 in Which Are Described Some of the Things that Happened*

to *Some of the Indians of California*, ed. Robert F. Heizer (Santa Barbara and Salt Lake City: Peregrine Smith, 1974), 255.

24. Carranco and Beard, *Genocide and Vendetta*, 61. Madley, "Patterns of Frontier Genocide," 178.

25. Carranco and Beard, *Genocide and Vendetta*, 59, 64–65, 82.

26. Benjamin Madley, "California's Yuki Indians: Defining Genocide in Native American History," *Western Historical Quarterly* 39 (2008): 179.

27. Miller, *Ukomno'm*, 66.

28. Madley, "California's Yuki Indians," 179. *The California Farmer*, March 27, 1861, carries a report that "300–400 bucks, squaws, and children have been killed by the whites," in *Exterminate Them! Written Accounts of the Murder, Rape and Enslavement of Native Americans during the California Gold Rush 1848–1868*, ed. Clifford E. Tratzer and Joel R. Hyer (East Lansing: Michigan State University Press, 1999), 130.

29. *Majority and Minority Report*, 6; my emphasis.

30. Ibid., 64.

31. Ibid., 3.

32. "Indian Troubles in Mendocino, *San Francisco Bulletin*, January 21, 1860, in Tratzer and Hyer, *Exterminate Them!*, 128.

33. Madley, "Patterns of Frontier Genocide," 180.

34. Carrasco and Beard, 90.

35. Mohamed Adhikari, *The Anatomy of a South African Genocide: The Extermination of the Cape San Peoples* (Athens: Ohio University Press, 2010), 33.

36. Ibid., 36.

37. Ibid., 38.

38. Adhikari, *The Anatomy*, 48.

39. Ibid., 52.

40. Anders Sparrman, cited in Adhikari, *The Anatomy*, 53.

41. Ibid., 54.

42. Ibid., 57.

43. Ibid., 62.

44. See Mohamed Adhikari, "'The Bushman is a Wild Animal to be Shot at Sight': Annihilation of the Cape Colony's Foraging Societies by Stock-Farming Settlers in the Eighteenth and Nineteenth Centuries," in Adhikari, *Genocide on Settler Frontiers*, 51–58.

45. Adhikari, *The Anatomy*, 77.

46. Ibid.

CHAPTER 5

1. James C. Scott, *Seeing Like a State: How Certain Schemes to Improve the Human Condition Have Failed* (New Haven: Yale University Press, 1998), 406; and Zygmunt Bauman, *Modernity and the Holocaust* (Ithaca, NY: Cornell University Press, 1989), 61–62.

2. Brian Porter, *When Nationalism Began to Hate: Imagining Modern Politics in Nineteenth Century Poland* (New York: Oxford University Press, 2000).

3. See, for example, Eric Weitz, *A Century of Genocide: Utopias of Race and Nation* (Princeton, NJ: Princeton University Press, 2003).

4. Isabel Hull, *Absolute Destruction: Military Culture and the Practices of War in Imperial Germany* (Ithaca, NY: Cornell University Press, 2005), 26–28. See also

Jürgen Zimmerer, *Genocide in German South-West Africa: The Colonial War of 1904–1908 and its Aftermath* (London: Merlin Press, 2008).

5. Cited in Jon Bridgman and Leslie J. Worley, "Genocide of the Hereros," in *Century of Genocide: Critical Essays and Eyewitness Accounts*, 2nd ed., ed. Samuel Totten, William S. Parsons, and Israel Charny (New York: Routledge, 2004), 27.

6. Cited in Hull, *Absolute Destruction*, 56.

7. Cited in ibid., 68.

8. "The German Operations: British Subjects as Combatants: Further Evidence: Women and Children Hanged and Shot: Sensational Allegations," September 25, 1905, *Cape Argus*, in *Words Cannot Be Found: German Colonial Rule in Namibia, An Annotated Reprint of the 1918 Blue Book*, ed. Jeremy Silvester and Jan-Bart Gewald (Leiden: Brill, 2003), 342.

9. See Vahakn N. Dadrian, *German Responsibility in the Armenian Genocide: A Review of the Historical Evidence of German Complicity* (Watertown, MA: Blue Crane, 1996).

10. See Norman M. Naimark, *Fires of Hatred: Ethnic Cleansing in Twentieth-Century Europe* (Cambridge, MA: Harvard University Press, 2001), 28.

11. See ibid., 23.

12. Ronald Grigor Suny, *"They Can Live in the Desert but Nowhere Else": A History of the Armenian Genocide* (Princeton, NJ: Princeton University Press, 2015).

13. Ibid., 246–80.

14. Fuat Dündar, "Pouring a People into the Desert: The 'Definitive Solution' of the Unionists to the Armenian Question," in *A Question of Genocide: Armenians and Turks at the End of the Ottoman Empire*, ed. Ronald G. Suny, Fatma Müge Göçek, and Norman M. Naimark (New York: Oxford University Press, 2011), 276–87.

15. Grigoris Balakian, *Armenian Golgotha: A Memoir of the Armenian Genocide, 1915–1918*, trans. Peter Balakian with Aris Sevag (New York: Vintage, 2009), 145.

16. Henry Morgenthau, *The Murder of a Nation* (New York: Armenian General Benevolent Society, 1974), 45–46.

17. Ibid., 66–68.

18. On the genocide of the Pontic Greeks, see Adam Jones, *Genocide: A Comprehensive Introduction*, 2nd ed. (London: Routledge, 2006), 244.

19. Cited in Naimark, *Fires of Hatred*, 57.

20. Max Domarus, *Hitler: Speeches and Proclamations 1932–1945. The Chronicle of a Dictatorship*, vol. 1, *1932–1934* (London: I. B. Tauris, 1990); emphasis in original.

21. Michael Burleigh and Wolfgang Wipperman, *The Racial State: Germany 1933–1945* (Cambridge: Cambridge University Press, 1993), 36–43. Michael Wildt, *Geschichte der Nationalsozialismus* (Göttingen: Vandenhoeck & Ruprecht, 2008).

22. Victor Klemperer, *I Will Bear Witness: A Diary of the Nazi Years, 1933–1941* (New York: Random House, 1999), 9.

23. Ibid., 12, 122.

24. For the beginnings of the Holocaust, see Christopher R. Browning, with contributions from Jürgen Matthäus, *The Origins of the Final Solution: The Evolution of Nazi Jewish Policy, September 1939–March 1942* (Lincoln: University of Nebraska Press, 2004).

25. *The Diary of Dawid Sierakowiak: Five Notebooks from the Łódź Ghetto*, ed. Alan Adelson, trans. Kamil Turkowski (New York and Oxford: Oxford University Press, 1996), 173.

26. Cited in Saul Friedländer, *Nazi Germany and the Jews, 1939–1945, The Years of Extermination* (New York: Harper Collins, 2007), 147.

27. Cited in Peter Longerich, *Joseph Goebbels, Biographie* (Munich: Siedler, 2010), 434, 462.

28. John-Paul Himka, "The Lviv Pogrom of 1941; The Germans, Ukrainian Nationalists, and the Carnival Crowd," *Canadian Slavonic Papers* 53, nos. 2, 3, 4 (June, September, December 2011): 209–38.

29. Jan T. Gross, *Neighbors: The Destruction of the Jewish Community in Jedwabne, Poland* (Princeton, NJ: Princeton University Press, 2001).

30. "The Commander of Security Police and Security Service, Kovno, December 1, 1941," in *Documents of Destruction: Germany and Jewry 1933–1945,* ed. Raul Hilberg (Chicago: Quadrangle Books, 1971), 46–57.

31. Ibid.

32. Ulrich Herbert, "Vernichtungspolitik: Neue Antworten und Fragen zur Geschichte des 'Holocausts,' " in *Nationalsozialistische Vernichtungspolitik 1939–1945: Neue Forschungen und Kontroversen*, ed. Ulricht Herbert (Frankfurt am Main: Fischer, 1998), 50; Christian Gerlach, "Deutsche Wirtschaftsinteressen, Besatzungspolitik und den Mord an den Juden in Weissrussland 1941–43," in *Nationalsozialistische Vernichtungspolitik*, 289, 313–15.

33. See Ian Kershaw, *Hitler 1939–1936: Hubris* (New York: W.W. Norton, 1998), 529–31.

34. Primo Levi, *Survival in Auschwitz* (New York: Touchstone, 1996), 90.

35. Timothy Snyder, *Bloodlands: Europe Between Hitler and Stalin* (New York: Basic Books, 2010), 253–58.

CHAPTER 6

1. See Norman M. Naimark, *Stalin's Genocides* (Princeton, NJ: Princeton University Press, 2010), 17–29.

2. Ben Kiernan, *The Pol Pot Regime: Race, Power, and Genocide in the Cambodia under the Khmer Rouge, 1975–79*, 3rd ed. (New Haven: Yale University Press, 2008), ix.

3. Frank Dikötter, *Mao's Great Famine: The History of China's Most Devastating Catastrophe, 1958–1962* (New York: Walker, 2002), 324–34; Andrew G. Walder, *China under Mao: A Revolution Derailed* (Cambridge, MA: Harvard University Press, 2015), 333–34, 364n63.

4. See Hiroaki Kuromiya, "Stalin in the Light of the Politburo Manuscripts," in *The Lost Politburo Transcripts*, ed. Paul Gregory and Norman M. Naimark (New Haven: Yale University Press, 2008), 41–57.

5. Cited in Lynne Viola, *Peasant Rebels under Stalin: Collectivization and the Culture of Peasant Resistance* (New York: Oxford University Press, 1996), 37.

6. Cited in Andrea Graziosi, *The Great Soviet Peasant War: Bolsheviks and Peasants, 1917–1933* (Cambridge, MA: Harvard University Ukrainian Research Institute, 1996), 49.

7. Cited in Lynne Viola, *The Unknown Gulag: The Lost World of Stalin's Special Settlements* (Oxford: Oxford University Press, 2007), 55.

8. Viola, *The Unknown Gulag*, 96; Anne Applebaum, *Gulag: A History* (New York: Doubleday, 2003), 102.

9. Cited in Nicolas Werth, *Cannibal Island: Death in the Siberian Gulag*, trans. by Steven Rendall (Princeton, NJ: Princeton University Press, 2007), 76–77.

10. Robert Gellately, *Lenin, Stalin, and Hitler: The Age of Social Catastrophe* (New York: Knopf, 2007), 227.

11. See Naimark, *Stalin's Genocides*, 73, for original citations.

12. Cited in Gellately, *Lenin, Stalin, and Hitler*, 234.

13. *Holodomor of 1932–33 in Ukraine: Documents and Materials* (Kyiv: Kyiv Mohyla Academy, 2008), 114–15.

14. See Naimark, *Stalin's Genocides,* pp. 81–86.

15. See Norman M. Naimark, *Fires of Hatred: Ethnic Cleansing in Twentieth-Century Europe* (Cambridge, MA: Harvard University Press, 2001), 92–107; Naimark, *Stalin's Genocides*, 80–98.

16. *The Diary of Georgi Dimitrov 1933–1939*, ed. Ivo Banac (New Haven: Yale University Press, 2003), 65.

17. Nicholas Werth, "The Crimes of the Stalin Regime: Outline for an Inventory and Classification," unpublished manuscript, in Naimark, *Stalin's Genocides*, 111.

18. Yu Dingyi at the National Party Congress, May 19, 1958, in Yang Jisheng, *Tombstone: The Great Chinese Famine, 1958–1962* , trans. by Stacy Mosher and Guo Jian, ed. Edward Friedman, Guo Jian, and Stacy Mosher (New York: Farrar, Straus and Giroux, 2012), 165.

19. Dikötter, *Mao's Great Famine*, 105–106.

20. "Chairman Mao's words at the Shanghai Conference, March 25, 1959," in *The Great Famine in China, 1958–1962: A Documentary History*, ed. Zhou Xun (New Haven: Yale University Press, 2012), 24–25.

21. "A study of cases of cannibalism in Linxia municipality ... March 3, 1961," in *The Great Famine in China*, 62.

22. Cited in Jisheng, *Tombstone*, 302.

23. Ibid., 347.

24. "Report on the problem of an increasing number of prostitutes and disorderly girls in the city ... August 1962," in *The Great Famine in China*, 135–36.

25. Dikötter, *Mao's Great Famine*, 258–59.

26. Jonathan Spence, *Mao Zedong: A Life* (New York: Penguin Books, 1999), 145.

27. *The Great Famine in China*, 175.

28. "A preliminary report to the Hunan Provincial Party Committee ... June 2, 1960," in *The Great Famine in China*, 32.

29. "A report by the Shizhu county branch of the Rectification Campaign Working Team ... January 1961," in *The Great Famine in China*, 33–34.

30. Dikötter, *Mao's Great Famine*, 297.

31. Ibid., 22.

32. "Speech by Comrade Liu Shaoqi [in Beijing], May 31, 1961," in *The Great Famine in China*, 164.

33. Dikötter, *Mao's Great Famine*, 335.

34. "Report on population figures in 1962 ... Sichuan Province Bureau of Public Security, February 23, 1963," in *The Great Famine in China*, 165.

35. Dikötter, *Mao's Great Famine*, 337.

36. "Documents on Consciousness (30-11-1976)," in *Ieng Sary's Regime: A Diary of the Khmer Rouge Foreign Ministry, 1976–79*, trans. by Phat Kosal and Ben Kiernan with Sorya Sim (New Haven: Yale Center for International and Area Studies, 1998), 29, www.yale.edu/egp/Iengsary.htm.

37. Mr. Sok Ros, 2.1.5.25, in *Genocide in Cambodia: Documents from the Trial of Pol Pot and Ieng Sary*, eds. Howard J. De Nike, John Quigley, and Kenneth J. Robinson (Philadelphia: University of Pennsylvania Press, 2000), 213.

38. "Document of the Central Committee of the Communist Party of Kampuchea Addressed to the Zone Administrative Committees After April 1975," 2.5.01, in De Nike, Quigley, and Robinson, *Genocide in Cambodia,* 379.

39. Mr. Men Khoeun, .2.01, in De Nike, Quigley, and Robinson, *Genocide in Cambodia*, 220.

40. Mr. Vang Pheap, 2.1.4.02, in De Nike, Quigley, and Robinson, *Genocide in Cambodia*, 158.

41. "View of the Situation of the Contemporary Kampuchean Revolution," in *Ieng Sary's Regime*, 32.

42. "The Current Political Tasks of Democratic Kampuchea," in *Ieng Sary's Regime*, 13.

43. Proum Duch Borannan, May 28, 1979, in De Nike, Quigley, and Robinson, *Genocide in Cambodia*, 85.

44. "Report on the General Political Tasks of the Party in the Northern Zone for the First Quarter of 1977 . . .," in De Nike, Quigley, and Robinson, *Genocide in Cambodia*, 387–88.

45. Mr. Ung Pech, 2.1.01, in De Nike, Quigley, and Robinson, *Genocide in Cambodia*, 81.

46. Loung Ung, *First They Killed My Father: A Daughter of Cambodia Remembers* (New York: Harper Collins, 2000), 82.

47. Kiernan, *The Pol Pot Regime*, 55.

48. Ibid., 296–97.

49. Ibid., 255.

50. Ibid., 273.

51. Ibid., 265–66.

52. Ibid., 458.

53. De Nike, Quigley, and Robinson, *Genocide in Cambodia*, 362.

54. Ung, *First They Killed My Father*, 67.

55. *Ieng Sary's Regime*, 3.

56. Cited in Samantha Power, *"A Problem from Hell": America in the Age of Genocide* (New York: Basic Books, 2002), 110.

CHAPTER 7

1. Kate Doyle and Peter Kornbluth, eds., "CIA and Assassinations: The Guatemala 1954 Documents," National Security Archive Electronic Briefing Book no. 4, www2.gwu.edu/~nsarchiv/NSAEBB/NSAEBB4/ (accessed August 21, 2013); Gerald K. Haines, "CIA and Guatemala Assassination Proposals 1952–1954," CIA History Staff Analyses, June 1955, www2.gwu.edu/~nsarchiv/NSAEBB/NSAEBB4/docs/doc01.pdf (accessed August 22, 2013), 1–2. Odd Arne Westad, *The Global Cold War* (Cambridge: Cambridge University Press, 2007), 147.

2. Doyle and Kornbluth, "CIA and Assassinations."

3. Thomas Hughes, INR, "Guatemala: A Counter-Insurgency Running Wild," October 23, 1963, in www2.gwu.edu/~nsarchiv/NSAEBB/NSAEBB11/docs/doc04.pdf.

4. Commission on Historical Clarification (CEH), *Guatemala: Memory of Silence*, 1999, www.documentcloud.org/documents/357870-guatemala-memory-of-silence-the-commission-for.html (accessed August 20, 2013), 26–27.

5. Benjamin Valentino, *Final Solutions: Mass Killing and Genocide in the 20th Century* (Ithaca, NY: Cornell University Press, 2004), 208.

6. Ibid., 209.

7. CEH, *Guatemala: Memory of Silence*, 21.

8. Valentino, *Final Solutions*, 210.

9. February 1992, CIA Secret Cable, www2.gwu.edu/~nsarchiv/NSAEBB/NSAEBB11/docs/doc14.pdf.

10. "Operation Sofia: Documenting Genocide in Guatemala," NSA Electronic Briefing book no. 297, December 2, 2009, www2.gwu.edu/~nsarchiv/NSAEBB/NSAEBB297/

11. Cited in Adam Jones, *Genocide: A Comprehensive Introduction*, 2nd ed. (London: Routledge, 2006), 142–43.

12. For the ubiquitous presence of rape, see "Summary of Genocide Proceedings before the Spanish Federal Court: Round One, February 4–8, 2008." For the killing of children, see especially the testimony of the reporter, Allan Nairn, Tuesday, February 5, 2008. www2.gwu.edu/~nsarchiv/guatemala/genocide/round1/summary1.pdf.

13. Testimony, Friday, February 8, 2008, in "Summary of Genocide Proceedings."

14. CEH, *Guatemala: Memory of Silence*, 34.

15. Valentino, *Final Solutions*, 210.

16. Testimony, February 4, 2008, in "Summary of Genocide Proceedings"; CEH, *Guatemala: Memory of Silence*, 35.

17. "The Final Battle: Rios Montt's Counterinsurgency Campaign: U.S. and Guatemalan Documents Describe the Strategy Behind Scorched Earth," May 9, 2013, ed. Kate Doyle, www2.gwu.edu/~nsarchiv/NSAEBB/NSAEBB425/.

18. "U.S. Policy in Guatemala," CIA Secret Cable, February 1983, www2.gwu.edu/~nsarchiv/NSAEBB/NSAEBB11/docs/doc18.pdf.

19. "Operation Sofia: Documenting Genocide in Guatemala," NSA Electronic Briefing Book no. 297, www2.gwu.edu/~nsarchiv/NSAEBB/NSAEBB425/.

20. CEH, *Guatemala: Memory of Silence*, 39–40.

21. *Foreign Relations of the United States (FRUS) 1964–68*, vol. 26: Indonesia: Malaysia-Singapore: Philippines (accessed through National Security Archive website August 26, 2013), www2.gwu.edu/~nsarchiv/NSAEBB/NSAEBB52/#FRUS.

22. Robert Cribb, "The Indonesian Massacres," in *Century of Genocide: Critical Essays and Eyewitness Accounts*, ed. Samuel Totten, William S. Parsons, and Israel Charny, 2nd ed. (New York: Routledge, 2004), 235–36.

23. *FRUS 1964–68*, "Telegram from the Department of State, October 22, 1965," 26:333, and "Memorandum from the Director of the Office of Southwest Pacific Affairs," 26:351.

24. "Memorandum from the Director of the Far East Region ([Admiral] Blouin) to the Assistant Secretary of Defense, October 4, 1965, *FRUS 1964–68*, 26:306.

25. Cribb, "The Indonesian Massacres," 237.

26. Leslie Dwyer and Degung Santikarma, "'When the World Turned to Chaos': 1965 and Its Aftermath in Bali, Indonesia," in *The Specter of Genocide: Mass Murder in Historical Perspective*, ed. Robert Gellately and Ben Kiernan (Cambridge: Cambridge University Press, 2003), 298.

27. Geoffrey Robinson, *The Dark Side of Paradise: Political Violence in Bali* (Ithaca, NY: Cornell University Press, 1995), 293.

28. John Roosa, *Pretext for Mass Murder: The September 30th Movement and Suharto's Coup d'Etat in Indonesia* (Madison: University of Wisconsin Press, 2006), 22.

29. The American Embassy took some credit for spreading "the story of PKI's guilt, treachery and brutality" by Voice of America broadcasts and otherwise. "Telegram from the Embassy in Indonesia to the Department of State," October 5, 1965, *FRUS 1964–65*, 26:307.

30. Dwyer and Santikarma, "'When the World Turned to Chaos,'" 294.

31. Robinson, *The Dark Side of Paradise*, 288.

32. Cited in ibid., 298.

33. "Editorial note," *FRUS 1964–68*, 26:338–39. "Intelligence Memorandum" CIA, Office of Current Intelligence, November 22, 1965, 26:375.

34. See the three firsthand accounts in Cribb, "The Indonesian Massacres," 249–60.

35. Robinson, *The Dark Side of Paradise*, 300.

36. Cited in Cribb, "The Indonesian Massacres," 53.

37. Clinton Fernandes, *The Independence of East Timor: Multi-Dimensional Perspectives—Occupation, Resistance, and International Political Activism* (Brighton: Sussex Academic Press, 2011), 47. Ben Kiernan, *Genocide and Resistance in Southeast Asia: Documentation, Denial & Justice in Cambodia and East Timor* (New Brunswick, NJ: Transaction, 2008), 277.

38. Kiernan, *Genocide and Resistance*, 111.

39. Ben Saul, "Was the Conflict in East Timor 'Genocide' and Why Does it Matter?" *Melbourne Journal of International Law* 2 (2001): 497–500.

40. Geoffrey Robinson, *"If You Leave Us Here We Will Die": How Genocide was Stopped in East Timor* (Princeton, NJ: Princeton University Press, 2010), 6.

41. Saul, "Was the Conflict in East Timor 'Genocide,' " 513.

42. Kiernan, *Genocide and Resistance*, 118–19.

43. Robinson, *"If You Leave Us Here,"* 54.

44. Cited in Kiernan, *Genocide and Resistance*, 128.

45. Fernandes, *The Independence of East Timor*, 49.

46. Saul, "Was the Conflict in East Timor 'Genocide,' " 515.

47. Robinson, *"If You Leave Us Here,"* 51.

48. Fernandes, *The Independence of East Timor*, 55.

49. Ibid., 55.

50. Andrea Katalin Molnar, *Timor Leste: Politics, History, and Culture* (London: Routledge, 2010), 50.

51. Robinson, *"If You Leave Us Here,"* 55.

52. Kiernan, *Genocide and Resistance*, 130.

53. Fernandes, *The Independence of East Timor*, 75.

54. Robinson, *"If You Leave Us Here,"* 66. The video of the Santa Cruz massacre is accessible at www.youtube.com/watch?v=8NYdGad-0bs.

55. Molnar, *Timor Leste*, 51–52.

56. Cited in Kiernan, *Genocide and Resistance*, 134.

CHAPTER 8

1. Cited in Marcus Tanner, *Croatia: A Nation Forged in War* (New Haven: Yale University Press, 1997), 88.

2. *The New York Times*, March 21, 1996.

3. *IWPR Tribunal Update*, February 2–6, 1998.

4. David Sheffer, *All the Missing Souls: A Personal History of the War Crimes Tribunals* (Princeton, NJ: Princeton University Press, 2010), 38.

5. United Nations General Assembly, "Report of the Secretary-General Pursuant to General Assembly Resolution 53.35," *The Fall of Srebrenica* (published report of the U.N.), November 15, 1999, 9.

6. *The New York Times*, February 7, 1993.

7. Roy Gutman, *A Witness to Genocide* (New York: Macmillan, 1993), 44–52. See also Louis Sell, "Slobodan Milosevic: A Political Biography," *Problems of Post-Communism* 46, no. 6 (November –December 1999): 25.

8. *IWPR Tribunal Update*, April 6–11 (1998).

9. He was convicted in 2008 for a series of crimes against humanity and was sentenced to 21 years in prison.

10. *IWPR Tribunal Update*, June 7–13, 1999.

11. Helsinki Watch, *War Crimes in Bosnia-Hercegovina*, vol. 2 (New York: Human Rights Watch, 1993), 21.

12. Catherine A. MacKinnon, "Turning Rape into Pornography: Turning Rape into Genocide," in *Mass Rape: The War against Women in Bosnia Herzegovina*, ed. Alexandra Stiglmayer, trans. Marion Faber (Lincoln: University of Nebraska Press, 1994), 73–81.

13. Norman M. Naimark, "Srebrenica in the History of Genocide: A Prologue," in *Memories of Mass Repression: Narrating Life Stories in the Aftermath of Atrocity*, ed. Nanci Adler, Selma Leydesdorff, et al. (New Brunswick, NJ: Transaction, 2009). See also Norman M. Naimark, *Fires of Hatred: Ethnic Cleansing in Twentieth-Century Europe* (Cambridge, MA: Harvard University Press, 2001), 164–65.

14. Chuck Sudetic, *Blood and Vengeance: One Family's Story of a War in Bosnia* (New York: W. W. Norton, 1998), 292–93.

15. "Dutch Peacekeepers Are Found Responsible for Deaths," *The New York Times*, September 6, 2013.

16. David Rohde, *Endgame: The Betrayal and Fall of Srebrenica, Europe's Worst Massacre since World War II* (New York: Farrar, Straus and Giroux, 1997), 313; Sudetic, *Blood and Vengeance*, 317; Jan Willem Honig and Norbert Both, *Srebrenica: Record of a War Crime* (New York: Penguin, 1996), 65.

17. Naimark, "Srebrenica," 13–14.

18. Mahmood Mamdani, *When Victims Become Killers: Colonialism, Nativism, and the Genocide in Rwanda* (Princeton, NJ: Princeton University Press, 2001), 76–103.

19. Liisa Malkki, *Purity and Exile: Violence, Memory, and National Cosmology among Hutu Refugees in Tanzania* (Chicago: University of Chicago Press, 1995), 91–93.

20. Scott Strauss, *The Order of Genocide: Race, Power, and War in Rwanda* (Ithaca, NY: Cornell University Press, 2006), 175.

21. Jacques Semelin, *Purify and Destroy: The Political Uses of Massacre and Genocide*, trans. Cynthia Schoch (London: Hurst, 2007), 123.

22. For the significance of the Tutsi–Hutu clashes in Burundi to the events in Rwanda, see Rene Lemarchand, "Genocide in the Great Lakes: Which Genocide? Whose Genocide?" *African Studies Review* 41, no. 1 (April 1998): 3.

23. Strauss, *The Order of Genocide*, 27–28.

24. Dallaire to Baril, January 11, 1994, National Security Archives, www2.gwu.edu/~nsarchiv/NSAEBB/NSAEBB53/rw011194.pdf.

25. *Defense Intelligence Report*, May 9, 1994, "Rwanda: The Rwandan Patriotic Front's Offensive," NSA, www2.gwu.edu/~nsarchiv/NSAEBB/NSAEBB53/rw050994.pdf.

26. ICTR, "The Prosecutor versus Akayesu," paragraphs 109, 110.

27. Ibid., paragraphs 100, 118.

28. Strauss, *The Order of Genocide*, 83.

29. ICTR, "The Prosecutor versus Akayesu," paragraph 732.

30. Some estimates are lower. See Strauss, *The Order of Genocide*, 51.

31. Philip Gourevitch, *"We Wish to Inform You that Tomorrow We Will Be Killed with Our Families": Stories from Rwanda* (New York: Picador, 1998), 220.

32. International Crisis Group, *Darfur Rising: Sudan's New Crisis*, ICG Africa Report no. 76, Nairobi/Brussels, March 25, 2004, 16.

33. *Report of the International Commission of Inquiry on Darfur to the United Nations Secretary-General*, January 25, 2005, 60.

34. David Scheffer, "Rape as Genocide," *The New York Times*, November 3, 2008.

35. *Documenting Atrocities in Darfur*, State Department Publication no. 11182, September 2004, http://2001-2009.state.gov/g/drl/rls/36028.htm

36. Ibid.

37. Interview conducted by Samuel Totten on June 6, 2007, in *Century of Genocide: Critical Essays and Eyewitness Accounts*, ed. Samuel Totten and William S. Parsons, 2nd ed. (New York: Routledge, 2004), 597–98.

38. *Report of the International Commission of Inquiry*, 75.

39. Ibid., 89.

40. Ibid., 91.

41. International Crisis Group, *Darfur Rising*, 17.

42. See Samuel Totten, *Genocide by Attrition: The Nuba Mountains of Sudan* (New Brunswick, NJ: Transaction, 2012).

43. Nicholas D. Kristof, "The Death Toll in Darfur," *The New York Times*, August 14, 2007.

44. Olivier Degomme and Debarati Guha-Sapir, "Patterns of Mortality Rates in Darfur Conflict," *Lancet* 375 (January 23, 2010): 297, www.thelancet.com.

45. U.S. Department of State Archive, "The Crisis in Darfur," Secretary Colin L. Powell, Testimony Before the Senate Foreign Relations Committee, September 9, 2004, http://2001-2009.state.gov/secretary/former/powell/remarks/36042.htm.

46. *Report of the International Commission of Inquiry*, 4.

CONCLUSION

1. Steven Pinker, *The Better Angels of Our Nature: Why Violence Has Declined* (New York: Penguin, 2011), 696.

Further Reading

Adhikari, Mohammed, ed. *Genocide on Settler Frontiers: When Hunter-Gatherers and Commercial Stock Farmers Clash*. Cape Town: University of Cape Town Press, 2014.

Bartov, Omer. *Mirrors of Destruction: War, Genocide, and Modern Identity*. New York: Oxford University Press, 2000.

Bloxham, Donald. *Genocide, the World Wars, and the Unweaving of Europe*. New York and Portland, OR: Valentine Mitchell, 2008.

Chalk, Frank, and Kurt Jonassohn. *The History and Sociology of Genocide: Analyses and Case Studies*. New Haven: Yale University Press, 1990.

Diamond, Jared. *Guns, Germs, and Steel: The Fates of Human Societies*. New York: W.W. Norton, 1999.

Diner, Dan. *Cataclysms: A History of the Twentieth Century from Europe's Edge*. Translated by William Templer with Joel Golb. Madison: University of Wisconsin Press, 2008.

Fredrickson, George M. *Racism: A Short History*. Princeton, NJ: Princeton University Press, 2002.

Gellately, Robert. *Lenin, Stalin, and Hitler: The Age of Social Catastrophe*. New York: Knopf, 2007.

Gellately, Robert, and Ben Kiernan, eds. *The Specter of Genocide: Mass Murder in Historical Perspective*. Cambridge: Cambridge University Press, 2003.

Jones, Adam. *Genocide: A Comprehensive Introduction*, 2nd ed. London: Routledge, 2006.

Kiernan, Ben. *Blood and Soil: A World History of Genocide and Extermination from Sparta to Darfur*. New Haven: Yale University Press, 2007.

Kiernan, Ben. *Genocide and Resistance in Southeast Asia: Documentation, Denial & Justice in Cambodia and East Timor*. New Brunswick, NJ: Transaction, 2008.

Kuper, Leo. *Genocide: Its Political Use in the Twentieth Century*. New Haven: Yale University Press, 1981.

Lemarchand, Rene, ed. *Forgotten Genocides: Oblivion, Denial and Memory*. Philadelphia: University of Pennsylvania Press, 2011.

Levene, Mark. *Genocide in the Age of the Nation-State*. Vol. 1, *The Meaning of Genocide*; Vol. 2, *The Rise of the West and the Coming of Genocide*. London: I.B. Taurus, 2005.

Levene, Mark. *The Crisis of Genocide*. Vol. 1, *Devastation: The European Rimlands 1912–1938*; Vol. 2, *Annihilation, The European Rimlands 1939–1953*. Oxford: Oxford University Press, 2013.

Lieberman, Benjamin. *Terrible Fate: Ethnic Cleansing in the Making of Modern Europe*. Chicago: Ivan R. Dee, 2004.

Madley, Benjamin. *An American Genocide: The United States and the Californian Indian Catastrope, 1846-1873*. New Haven: Yale University Press, 2016.

Mann, Michael. *The Dark Side of Democracy: Explaining Ethnic Cleansing*. Cambridge: Cambridge University Press, 2005

Melson, Robert F. *Revolution and Genocide: On the Origins of the Armenian Genocide and the Holocaust.* Chicago: University of Chicago Press, 1992.

Midlarsky. Manus I. *The Killing Trap: Genocide in the Twentieth Century.* Cambridge: Cambridge University Press, 2005.

Moses, A. Dirk. *Empire, Colony, Genocide: Conquest, Occupation, and Subaltern Resistance in World History.* New York: Berghahn Books, 2010.

Naimark, Norman M. *Fires of Hatred: Ethnic Cleansing in Twentieth-Century Europe.* Cambridge, MA: Harvard University Press, 2001.

Pinker, Steven. *The Better Angels of our Nature: Why Violence Has Declined.* New York: Penguin, 2011.

Power, Samantha. *"A Problem from Hell": America and the Age of Genocide.* New York: Basic Books, 2002.

Rummel, R. J. *Death by Government.* New Brunswick, NJ: Transaction, 2004.

Semelin, Jacques. *Purify and Destroy: The Political Uses of Massacre and Genocide.* Translated by Cynthia Schoch. London: Hurst, 2007.

Sheffer, David. *All the Missing Souls: A Personal History of the War Crimes Tribunals.* Princeton, NJ: Princeton University Press, 2012.

Snyder, Timothy. *Bloodlands: Europe Between Hitler and Stalin.* New York: Basic Books, 2010.

Suny, Ronald Grigor. *"They Can Live in the Desert but Nowhere Else": A History of the Armenian Genocide.* Princeton, NJ: Princeton University Press, 2015.

Totten, Samuel, William S. Parsons, and Israel Charny, eds. *Century of Genocide: Critical Essays and Eyewitness Accounts,* 2nd ed. New York: Routledge, 2004.

Valentino, Benjamin. *Final Solutions: Mass Killing and Genocide in the 20th Century.* Ithaca, NY: Cornell University Press, 2004.

Weitz, Eric. *A Century of Genocide: Utopias of Race and Nation.* Princeton, NJ: Princeton University Press, 2003.

Websites

International Criminal Tribunal for the former Yugoslavia (ICTY) and for the International Criminal Tribunal for Rwanda (ICTR)
www.icty.org/
www.unictr.org/en/tribunal

The ICTY and the ICTR, ad hoc tribunals established by the United Nations, are responsible for trying criminals related to war crimes and genocide committed in the former Yugoslavia and Rwanda. Their websites include information about past and ongoing cases, briefings about the trials and the accused, documentaries about the Tribunals' work, and other outreach information. The ICTR was closed on December 31, 2015, but continues to maintain a website.

International Crisis Group
www.crisisgroup.org/

The International Crisis Group works to increase international understanding and responds to atrocities committed around the world. The website includes reports, briefings, crisis watch materials, interviews, and alerts about atrocity crimes. Their three-tiered strategy includes field research and analysis, policy recommendations, and advocacy.

International Network of Genocide Scholars
www.inogs.com

The association of scholars was founded in 2005 in Berlin to foster interdisciplinary research and analysis on diverse aspects of genocide. It supports the *Journal of Genocide Research*, as well as conferences and symposia involving genocide tudies.

The Enough Project
www.enoughproject.org/

The Enough Project was founded by activists and policymakers concerned with the ongoing atrocities in Africa. The organization aims to "build leverage for peace and justice in Africa" by countering violent organizations. Its website includes reports on mass atrocities in Africa, news updates on ongoing conflicts, and information on Enough Project advocacy.

UN Office of the Special Advisor on the Prevention of Genocide
www.un.org/en/preventgenocide/adviser/

The role of the UN Special Advisor on the Prevention of Genocide is to "act as a catalyst to raise awareness of the causes and dynamics of genocide, to alert relevant actors where there is a risk of genocide, and to advocate and mobilize for appropriate action." The Office's website includes information on U.N. action to prevent genocide, international law regarding genocide and mass atrocities, and actions the office takes to prevent genocide.

United States Holocaust Memorial Museum (USHMM)
www.ushmm.org/

The United States Holocaust Memorial Museum is a living memorial to the Holocaust, founded in order to "inspire citizens and leaders worldwide to confront hatred, prevent genocide, and promote human dignity." In addition to the museum on the National Mall in Washington, D.C., USHMM maintains vast online resources. These include the Holocaust Encyclopedia; educational materials on the Holocaust for teachers, students and professionals; and archives of primary source documents, including pictures, maps, and survivor testimony.

United to End Genocide
http://endgenocide.org/
United to End Genocide is a coalition of organizations such as the Save Darfur Coalition, Genocide Intervention Network, and the Sudan Divestment Task Force, among others, who work to prevent genocide and mass atrocities around the world. The website includes information about the definition of genocide, reports on modern-day atrocities, conflict updates, and how to get involved in activism.

Yale Genocide Studies Program
http://gsp.yale.edu/
The Genocide Studies Program at Yale's MacMillan Center for International and Area Studies was founded in 1998 to expand the work of the university's Cambodian Genocide Program. The website includes case studies, audio and visual resources, scholarly articles relating to genocide, transcripts of trials and testimonies, and maps and satellite images of genocides. The GSP also conducts research projects on conflicts such as the Nazi Holocaust, the Srebrenica genocide, Darfur, and colonial genocides.

Acknowledgments

The field of genocide studies has grown exponentially over the past two decades, leading to the publication of a vast quantity of academic studies, sometimes comparative and world historical in character, but mostly related to single cases, such as the Holocaust, the Armenian genocide, or the Rwandan genocide. I am deeply indebted to this literature, without which it would have been impossible to write this study. Given the character of the book—short, synoptic, and selective—I could neither cite all the literature that I consulted nor engage in historiographical discussions with it. At the same time, it is important that I give credit to the important contributions to my thinking of at least a few of those authors whose works were central to my "world historical" approach: Mohammed Adhikari, Donald Bloxham, Mark Levene, Dirk Moses, William Schabas, Jacques Semelin, Eric Weitz, and, most crucially, Ben Kiernan.

In more than four decades of research and writing, I have been extraordinarily fortunate in having friends and colleagues who have willingly read and commented on my work. This was especially important for this book, since I could not possibly master cultures and time periods so widely dispersed from my own modern Russian and European competencies. For their willingness to read and critique sections on their fields of expertise, I thank Donald Emmerson, Jorge Ramón González, Caitlin Monroe, Andrew Walder, and Steven Weitzman. I am also beholden to those dear friends and long-time colleagues who commented on the manuscript in full: David Holloway and Ronald Suny. The two readers for Oxford University Press were diligent, helpful and, in one case, sufficiently sharp-tongued to force me to rethink how I presented some of the material. Nancy Toff, the Oxford editor of the series, gave of her precious time to go through the manuscript, for which I am deeply grateful. My wife and partner in Clio's labors, Katherine Jolluck, proved once again to be an extraordinarily helpful critic of my work. Lukas Dovern, a Stanford Ph.D. student, aided with maps and illustrations, as did Alina Utrata, a talented Stanford undergraduate.

I also want to acknowledge those institutions that have provided a home for this work and interested colleagues to share my ideas with: the Center for Advanced Study in the Behavioral Sciences, the American Academy in Berlin, the Center for International Security and Cooperation, the Freeman-Spogli Institute, the Hoover Institution (with its Archives and Library), and Stanford's Department of History. Without the time off, the lively seminars, and the many informal conversations, this work could neither have gotten off the ground nor been finished.

This book was inspired by six years of teaching a Freshman Seminar at Stanford on "A World History of Genocide." I want to thank those students—every one of them—for their questions, their comments, their challenges, and their papers. In particular, I want to thank the course assistants—Caitlin Monroe, Melanie Lange, and Alina Utrata—for their varied contributions to this book, as well as to the course. Students who have worked with me in Stanford's summer research college in International Relations have also enriched my understanding of various aspects of the history of genocide and problems of intervention. I dedicate this book to all those Stanford undergraduates whose passion for creating a world without genocide leaves one with a glimmer of hope in a pretty dark historical landscape.

Norman M. Naimark is the Robert
and Florence McDonnell Professor
of East European Studies and Senior
Fellow of the Hoover Institution
and the Institute of International
Studies at Stanford University. His
books include *The Russians in
Germany: The History of The Soviet
Zone of Occupation, 1945–1949;
Fires of Hatred: Ethnic Cleansing in
20th Century Europe;* and *Stalin's
Genocides.*

Index

Berlin, 68, 71, 76, 82
Béziers, 30–31, 33
Bibileo, 120
Bible, 7–12, 26, 29, 45, 76
Bitlis, 75
Boers, 66
Boesman (Bosjesman), 60
Boghazliyan, 73
Bohemond of Taranto, 27
Bolivia, 46
Bolsheviks, 80, 86, 88, 91
bombings, 98, 106, 108, 118, 125, 128
Bora, 139
borders 67, 76, 90, 107, 124, 132, 139
Bosnia, Bosnians, 124, 126–131,
    139–141, 144
Boxer Rebellion, 69
Brantas, 114
Brezhnev, Leonid, 104
British, 5, 32, 48–52, 54, 62–64, 66, 71, 75,
    92, 120
Buddhism, 101–102
Bufo, 121
Buikarin, 120
Bukhara, 20–21
Burundi, Burundians, 131–133, 140
Bush, George W., 140
Bushmanland, Bushman, 60–64
Byzantine, 25, 27

Cajamarca, 44–46
California, 56–59
Cambodians, 86, 97–103, 143
Camp David, 116
Canaan, 9, 26
Canadians, 132
cannibalism, 7, 27, 89, 93–94, 97
Cape Argus, 69
Cape, Cape Town, 60–64, 66. See also San
capitalism, 76, 98, 104, 143
captive, captivity , 9, 38–39, 56, 68,
    111, 121
Carcassonne, 30–32
Caribbean, 34, 37, 39–40, 46, 56
Carnegie Peace Foundation, 2
Carolingian empire, 26
Carthagians, 5, 7, 13–14, 20
Castillo Armas, Carlos, 105–106
Cathar, 29–34
Catholics, 25–26, 30–32, 34, 43, 47, 102,
    115, 120–121
Cato, Marcus Porcius, 5, 13–14
Caucasus, 91
Ceniza. See Operation Ashes
Chad, 138–140
Cham Roa, 100, 102–103
Charles V, 37, 41, 44
Che Guevara, 105
Chechens, 91

Chelmno, 83
Cherokees, 56
Chhnang, 101
children, 4, 9–12, 14–16, 19–21, 28, 31,
    35, 40–42, 47, 50, 55–56, 58–59, 61–62,
    64, 66–69, 73, 78–79, 81, 87, 90, 94–95,
    100–101, 106–110, 118–121, 126–127,
    129, 134
Chinese, 18–19, 24, 33, 86, 92–93, 96–97,
    101–103, 110–111, 114, 117
Cholula, 41–42, 44
Christianity, 2, 11, 17, 25–29, 31–32, 37–38,
    40, 62–63, 71, 84, 107, 114
CIA, 105–107
Cilicia, 75
civilians, 16–17, 24, 48, 106–107, 109–110,
    113, 115, 118, 125, 128, 134–135
Clarification, the Commission of, 106,
    109–110
Clermont, 26
collaboration, 72, 80, 82, 91, 118
collectivization, 87–89, 92
Coloma, 57
colonialism, 5, 12, 37, 40, 48, 50–52,
    54–56, 60–64, 66–68, 105, 111, 116, 131,
    143–144
Columbus, Christopher, 34–40, 47–48, 145
Comanche, 56
commanders, 11, 40, 73, 81, 107–108, 113,
    127, 129
commandos, 61–63, 81, 106
Commissariat, 80
communism, 76, 79–80, 86–87, 89–93, 95,
    97–99, 101, 103–113, 115–119, 121–122,
    124, 143
Comrade Duch. See Kaing Guek Eav
concentration camps, 143
Congo, 135–136, 141, 144
Connecticut, 56
conquistadors, 34, 40, 44–48
conspiracy, 76, 111–112
Constantinople, 25–26, 72
conventions, 1–4, 86, 103, 143
convicts, 50–55, 107, 117, 126
corpses, 22–23, 28–29, 36, 80, 83, 108–109,
    112, 114, 130
Corrective Labor Camps, 88
Cortés, Hernán, 34, 40–44, 47
corvée,37. See also encomienda
coup, 97, 105–107, 109, 112, 116
CPK (Communist Party of Kampuchea), 97
creoles, 50, 54
Crimea, 91
crimes, 1–4, 23, 33, 92, 99, 123–124, 126,
    135, 137, 140
criminals, 3, 55, 60, 72, 123, 137, 140, 144
Croats, 124–126
Crusade, 17, 25–34, 36, 39, 47
Cuba, Cubans, 39–41, 104, 107

Printed in the USA/Agawam, MA
March 2, 2018

670721.007